How Mediation Works

Theory, Research, and Practice

To Andrew
Kellogg conflict management program
Jeanne Brett
December 2019

How Mediation Works will be the "go to" book for people who want to better resolve their own conflicts, as well as for professional mediators to improve their craft. Easy to read, this book will prepare you to maximize success in a mediation by teaching you how mediation works from the inside. I recommend *How Mediation Works* to law students, mediation trainees, experienced mediators, collaborative professionals and others who want to get their skills to the next level, and to my clients who need to resolve conflict in their lives. I am proud to have *How Mediation Works* be part of my office's Client Library and a recommended book for those seeking my mediation training.

— Forrest S. Mosten, Adjunct Professor,
UCLA School of Law; mediator; mediation trainer;
author of Mediation Career Guide (2001),
Complete Guide to Mediation, 2nd Edition (2015)

As a seasoned civil trial lawyer who has embraced, when conducted competently, mediation as the most effective alternative dispute resolution vehicle, I commend *How Mediation Works* to *all* civil trial lawyers and mediators — seasoned and neophytes alike. The authors have dedicated a significant portion of their professional lives to teaching mediation and negotiation, and should be applauded for reducing their expertise to a writing that will become the bible for all who find themselves in the world of mediation. The book accurately delineates the roles of the mediator, lawyers and litigants in a cogent, practical, and easy-to-read fashion. It is, in my opinion, a must-read for all of us who truly aspire to successfully participate in the mediation process.

— Thomas A. Demetrio, Founding Partner,
Corboy and Demetrio, Chicago, IL.
Past President, Chicago Bar Association,
Illinois Trial Lawyers Association

The role played by a manager in resolving workplace conflict, whether between peers or subordinates, bears a close relationship to the mediation process described in *How Mediation Works*. Like a mediator, the manager seeks to facilitate an agreement that contributes to each party's satisfaction and, in turn, strengthens their relationship. The authors of *How Mediation Works* — each with decades of hands-on and research-guided expertise in achieving these ends — explain with refreshing clarity the processes that enable conflicts to be positively resolved. For these reasons, the advice provided (in plain English, not "legalize") in *How Mediation Works* should be required reading for both managers and management students.

— Debra L. Shapiro, Clarice Smith
Professor of Management & Organization,
Robert H. Smith School of Business, University of Maryland;
President, Academy of Management (2015–2016)

In this clearly written guide to mediation, the authors present central concepts of dispute resolution with refreshing simplicity, accompanied by a sound theoretical approach based on decades of research and mediation practice. Disputants as well as mediators, new and experienced alike, will find this book valuable reading.

— *William Ury, co-author, Getting to Yes*
(world-wide best-seller on negotiation). Co-founder,
Harvard Program on Negotiation. Mediator of conflicts
ranging from Kentucky coal mine strikes to ethnic wars in
the Middle East, the Balkans, and the former Soviet Union.

How Mediation Works is a short, comprehensive, well-written, and easily accessible book on mediation for both practitioners and students. It covers a wide range of mediation contexts, including family, neighborhood, employment, commercial, and environmental disputes. *How Mediation Works* includes chapters on dispute resolution, the mediation process, mediation techniques, impasse resolution, and how to get into the field of mediation. These will be of interest to both experienced and new practitioners. In addition, *How Mediation Works* is well suited as a textbook for both ADR courses and mediation training programs. Thanks to the authors for providing such a useful book. I intend to add it to my list of recommended books immediately.

— *Zena D. Zumeta, Mediator and mediation trainer,*
Ann Arbor, MI. President, Mediation Training & Consultation
Institute and The Collaborative Workplace.
Former president, Academy of Family Mediators

How Mediation Works is a first-rate book by authors with impressive credentials as mediators and mediation researchers. In my current role as a full-time mediator, I was particularly impressed by their recognition that the mediator's function is not necessarily to assist the disputants in reaching settlement, but rather to aid them in determining whether the best agreement available in mediation — which the mediator will assist in developing — sufficiently satisfies their interests to be acceptable, when compared to the best outcome reasonably to be expected in litigation. Viewed from this perspective, the mediator is not a deal-maker, but a helper to each party. The ultimate choice whether or not to settle is up to them, and the mediator who has done all he can to assist each in making that choice has fully satisfied his obligation — regardless of whether or not they choose to settle. Settlement, in other words, is not the criterion of successful mediation.

— *Hon. Morton Denlow, Attorney 1972–1996;*
Magistrate Judge, U.S. District Ct. (ND IL),
1996–2012 (ret.); Mediator, Judicial Arbitration
and Mediation Service (JAMS) 2012.

Resolution Systems Institute values straightforward, technically accurate information about mediation in our work to develop, administer and evaluate mediation programs. This is especially important in cases such as mortgage foreclosure, child protection and small claims, where mediation promotes access to justice for participants. *How Mediation Works* provides a valuable new source of that kind of information.

— *Susan M. Yates, Mediator and Executive Director,*
Resolution Systems Institute, Chicago, IL.

How Mediation Works

Theory, Research, and Practice

By

Stephen B. Goldberg
Professor Emeritus, Pritzker School of Law,
Northwestern University, Chicago, IL, USA

Jeanne M. Brett
Professor, Kellogg School of Management,
Northwestern University, Evanston, IL, USA

Beatrice Blohorn-Brenneur
Mediator, Council of Europe, Judge (ret.),
Paris, France

With

Nancy H. Rogers
Professor Emeritus, Moritz College of Law,
Ohio State University, Columbus, OH, USA

United Kingdom – North America – Japan – India – Malaysia – China

Emerald Publishing Limited
Howard House, Wagon Lane, Bingley BD16 1WA, UK

First edition 2017

British Library Cataloguing in Publication Data
A catalogue record for this book is available from the British Library

ISBN: 978-1-78714-223-7 (Print)
ISBN: 978-1-78714-222-0 (Online)
ISBN: 978-1-78714-723-2 (Epub)

ISOQAR certified
Management System,
awarded to Emerald
for adherence to
Environmental
standard
ISO 14001:2004.

Certificate Number 1985
ISO 14001

INVESTOR IN PEOPLE

About the Authors

Beatrice Blohorn-Brenneur is Mediator for the Counsel of Europe. She instituted mediation at the Grenoble Court of Appeals, where she mediated hundreds of cases. She is the President of the International Conference of Mediation for Justice (CIMJ), the European Association of Judges for Mediation (GEMME), and GEMME-France. Judge Brenneur has written extensively about mediation, and for many years provided mediation training to judges at the French National Judicial College.

Jeanne M. Brett is the DeWitt W. Buchanan, Jr. Distinguished Professor of Dispute Resolution and Organizations, Kellogg School of Management, Northwestern University, Evanston, IL. Brett's research has focused on mediation, mediator behavior, and disputant satisfaction with mediation compared to other dispute resolution processes. She has also studied how culture affects negotiation and dispute resolution. She is the author of numerous journal articles, negotiation teaching materials, and award winning books: *Negotiating Globally*, now in its third edition, and *Getting Disputes Resolved* with William Ury and Stephen Goldberg. She initiated Kellogg's MBA courses in negotiations in 1981, and in cross-cultural negotiations in 1994. She was a founder of Kellogg's Dispute Resolution Research Center in 1986, and Center director, 1986–2016.

Stephen B. Goldberg is Professor of Law Emeritus at the Pritzker School of Law, Northwestern University. He has served as a mediator since 1980, mediating hundreds of disputes, including disputes between neighbors, disputes between divorcing spouses, employer-employee disputes, labor-management disputes, and domestic and international commercial disputes with billions of dollars at stake. Professor Goldberg began teaching mediation to law students in 1981, and has conducted mediation training classes for hundreds of beginning mediators, as well as for advocates in mediation. He is the founder and president of Mediation

Research & Education Project, Inc., a not-for-profit corporation that promotes mediation of labor-management disputes, and trains disputing parties on how to be successful in mediation. Professor Goldberg has published numerous articles on negotiation, mediation, and dispute systems design, as well as the following books – *Dispute Resolution: Negotiation, Mediation, Arbitration, and Other Processes* (with Frank E. A. Sander, Nancy H. Rogers, and Sarah R. Cole); and *Getting Disputes Resolved: Designing Systems to Cut the Costs of Conflict* (with Jeanne M. Brett and William L. Ury).

Nancy H. Rogers (author of Chapter 5, *Mediation and the Law*) has practiced, taught, and written in the mediation field for more than 30 years. She is the Emeritus Moritz Chair in Alternative Dispute Resolution at the Ohio State University Moritz College of Law, where she also directs the Program on Law and Leadership. She served as reporter for the Uniform Mediation Act. She is a co-author of a three-volume treatise, *Mediation: Law, Policy & Practice*, which is updated annually and is a database on Westlaw. In addition, she is a co-author of three law school textbooks: *Dispute Resolution: Negotiation, Mediation, Arbitration and Other Processes, Designing Systems and Processes for Managing Disputes*, and *A Student's Guide to Mediation and the Law*. Her recent article on mediation within divided communities garnered the 2015 CPR Professional Article Award. She was Dean of the Ohio State University Moritz College of Law (2001–2008) and Ohio Attorney General (2008–2009).

Contents

Acknowledgments

Many people provided assistance to us in conceiving and writing *How Mediation Works*. We particularly want to thank Nancy Rogers, who, in addition to contributing the chapter on Mediation and the Law, provided feedback and advice for improvement on every other chapter. Special thanks are also due to Susan Yates, who helped us understand those areas of mediation with which she is more familiar than are we, and who provided both constructive criticism and advice on all aspects of the book. Bill Hobgood suggested that we provide advice to those who are interested in becoming mediators, and Chapter 6 is the result of that wise suggestion. Jessica Nelson helped us immensely with formatting, and Melissa Cryder helped with a myriad of administrative and clerical tasks.

Finally, we wish to think the anonymous reviewers who helped us in many ways to improve a book that we – wrongly – thought was complete when it went out for review.

Introduction

Mediation is a dispute resolution process in which a neutral third party, who does not have the authority to impose an outcome on disputing parties (as does a judge) seeks to assist them in resolving their dispute.

This book is for people who want to learn more about how mediation works. Some will be *mediation providers* – mediators and would-be mediators. People who are already mediators should find the book useful as a quick review of their role in the mediation process. They may also benefit from the dialogues that illustrate how they might approach, for example, a disputant's unwillingness to make the first offer, or concerns about the confidentiality of mediation. Mediators practicing in the United States will also find the review of mediation and the law in Chapter 5 valuable in ensuring that they act consistently with the law on such matters as the confidentiality of mediation, the mediator's obligation to act impartially, and the preservation of the disputants' free choice whether or not to settle in mediation.

This book is also for judges and arbitrators who seek to mediate some disputes, rather than decide them. Judges and arbitrators may also find the book useful in developing criteria for deciding whether certain disputants should be encouraged to seek a resolution in mediation rather than in court or arbitration.

An important category of readers consists of those who want to learn about how mediation works because they are *mediation users* – those who will or may participate in mediation. Among these are disputants and those who represent disputants in mediation – sometimes lawyers, sometimes people who are not lawyers, but are knowledgeable about the context in which the dispute arises, such as union representatives or human resources personnel. This book provides them with an understanding about what mediators do and why they do it.

Managers, who often find themselves involved in disputes between peers or subordinates, may benefit from the book's advice on facilitating the resolution of disputes. Although managers are not mediators in the pure sense — mediators do not have authority to impose an outcome on disputes and managers often do — managers will find that they can use many of the mediation techniques here discussed. Managers may also fall into the category of mediation users when their organizations are involved in a dispute with another organization or individual, such as customers or suppliers.

Finally, there is a category of readers — *mediation learners* — who do not have an immediate interest in providing or using mediation, but want to learn about how mediation works because of its growing use to resolve a wide range of disputes.

To address readers with such different reasons for their interest in mediation, we could have written two, if not three, separate books. Instead, we chose to write a single book addressing all these potential readers. We did so because we assumed that not just mediators and would-be mediators, but also mediation users and those curious about mediation would be interested in how mediation works — which is what this book is about.

Because of the variety of audiences for this book, you may find some material that is of direct interest to you and some that will be only indirectly interesting. Skip the latter if you wish, but the book is sufficiently short that you can easily read it all, and in doing so enlarge and deepen your understanding of mediation.

Chapter 1 introduces three different approaches to dispute resolution. A disputing party, in seeking a favorable outcome to a dispute, may rely upon its power (physical, economic, or psychological), its rights (normally based on law or contract), or its interests (needs, wants, concerns). Chapter 2 provides advice to disputing parties on selecting a dispute resolution process suitable for their dispute, pointing out that courts and arbitrators focus solely on rights, while mediation can — and often does — focus primarily on the parties' interests — their needs and concerns — while not ignoring their rights and power.

Chapter 3 focuses on how to make mediation work effectively. It discusses why some disputants and/or their lawyers are reluctant to mediate, and suggests how to address that reluctance. It also addresses the practical aspects of getting started with mediation — selecting a mediator, developing the ground rules for mediation, and many others. Chapter 3 also describes the mediator's role at each step of the mediation process: (1) aiding the parties in discovering their interests and priorities; (2) using those interests and priorities to assist the parties in developing potential settlements; (3) encouraging the parties to make the best settlement offers possible; and (4) aiding each party in comparing the best agreement available in mediation with the best outcome it can reasonably expect outside mediation.

Chapter 4 turns to the most common difficulties encountered in mediation, and provides suggestions for overcoming those difficulties. These include the parties' inability to reach agreement; the reluctance of each party to make the first offer; highly emotional parties; parties focused narrowly on who is right and who is wrong; and steps to take when the mediation appears to be at an impasse.

Because so much mediation occurs in relationship to a pending or potential lawsuit, Chapter 5 examines the relationship between mediation and the law. Among the topics treated in Chapter 5 are legal protections for the confidentiality of mediation; the disputants' obligations to attend and engage in mediation; the mediator's obligation to act impartially and with clarity and integrity; preservation of the disputants' free choice whether or not to settle in mediation; and the protection of the judicial system's role and reputation.

In Chapter 6, we provide frank advice for readers who think they would like to be mediators. We begin by quoting experienced mediators on the psychological rewards and social value of serving as a mediator. The chapter then focuses on the difficulty of making mediation a full-time career — primarily a greater supply of would-be mediators than demand for mediation services. Chapter 6 concludes with advice on overcoming that difficulty. Here we discuss the importance of taking one or more basic mediation training courses; the value of getting appropriate credentials (often, but not always, a law degree); developing a marketing plan; and keeping up with developments in mediation by joining mediator organizations and reading about mediation (with suggestions for both).

One final note to those readers who are primarily interested in the practice of mediation in countries outside the United States. Chapter 5 is admittedly limited to the relationship between mediation and the law in the United States, and Chapter 6 deals with becoming a mediator in the United States. On the other hand, we believe that Chapters 1–4, with their focus on interests, rights, and power as differing approaches to resolving disputes are equally valuable in other countries and cultures. So, too, we think that our analysis of the advantages of interest-based mediation and the roles of the mediator and the parties in interest-based mediation will be as useful to mediation providers, users, and learners in other countries and cultures as in the United States.

Stephen B. Goldberg

Jeanne M. Brett

Beatrice Blohorn-Brenneur

Nancy H. Rogers (Chapter 5)

1 Conflict, Disputes, and Their Resolution

Conflict and Disputes

The word "conflict" comes from the Latin word "confligere," which means to collide. Conflict is a collision of viewpoints or opinions between individuals or groups. A dispute is a specific type of conflict in which one party makes a claim on another, who rejects the claim, giving rise to a dispute. For example, there is considerable conflict between government environmental protection agencies that are responsible for protecting public land, and recreational users such as motorcyclists and RV owners who want to use public land. When an RV owner requests a permit to drive a vehicle into a public park for an overnight stay, and that request is denied, a dispute arises. Conflict may also exist between a husband and wife who have different views on how limited family funds should be spent; that conflict becomes a dispute when the husband proposes buying a new car and the wife objects.

Many people think that conflict and its expression in disputes are harmful. But, if well-managed, disputes can have constructive consequences. Disputes can motivate the parties to air their different interests, make difficult trade-offs, and reach agreements that satisfy the essential needs of each. A dispute that ends with a mutually satisfactory agreement, reached in a constructive manner, can solidify an existing relationship or serve as the basis of a new relationship.

1

There are three ways of trying to resolve disputes: focus on interests, rights, and power (Ury, Brett, & Goldberg, 1993).

Three Approaches to Dispute Resolution

POWER

A party using power to resolve a dispute seeks to prevail over the other party by using force — physical, economic, or psychological. An example of physical force would be a civil rights group blocking access to a restaurant believed to be discriminating in hiring; economic force would be the civil rights group organizing a consumer boycott of the restaurant; psychological force would be a member of the civil rights group refusing to talk to one of his friends until he stopped patronizing the restaurant. Threats to take harmful action if one's demands are not met are another use of power.

Determining which party is the more powerful without engaging in a potentially destructive power contest is difficult. This is because power is largely a matter of perception and each party's perception of its own and the other party's power may differ. Additionally, once a power struggle has begun, it can easily spiral out of control as each party invests more and more resources for fear of losing a decisive battle. The restaurant believed by the civil rights group to be discriminating may, for example, engage high-priced lawyers to seek millions of dollars in a defamation action designed to bankrupt the civil rights group. The latter, in turn, may seek to persuade suppliers not to do business with the restaurant. In the end, a power contest results in costs for both parties, even if one capitulates.

RIGHTS

Another way to resolve disputes is to rely on an independent standard with perceived legitimacy or fairness, such as the law or a contract between the parties, to determine which party is "right." A problem with this approach is that rights are rarely clear. One party relies on a law that supports its position; the other party relies on a different law or a different interpretation of the first law. To resolve the question of whose rights standard or interpretation should prevail, the parties often need to turn to a third party, an arbitrator or judge, to make a binding decision.

Involving a third party decision-maker is frequently a costly and time-consuming procedure. Furthermore, the loser may only grudgingly comply with the third-party's decision, leading to further disputes. Finally, a conclusion that one party is right and the other wrong may end their existing relationship and the prospect of any future relationship. Think of the number of divorced couples, who, after a bitter court fight over child custody, are soon back in court because they cannot cooperate on some new child-related issue.

INTERESTS

Interests are peoples' needs, desires, concerns, or fears – the things they care about or want. Interests underlie people's positions – the tangible items they say they want when they make or reject claims. Reconciling interests is not easy. It involves probing for deep-seated concerns, determining which interests are more important than others, devising creative solutions that reconcile interests, and making trade-offs and concessions. But, interest-based agreements are possible in many disputes. Recall the quarrel between husband and wife about whether to spend money for a new car. Suppose that his underlying interest was to impress his friends and hers was reliable transportation. An interest-based solution might be to buy a high end, but less expensive, used car with a long-term warranty, so satisfying the wife's interest in reliable transportation and the husband's interest in impressing his friends. In the land use permit dispute, both the government agency and the user groups may have an interest in conserving the park for future use. As a result, the agency may agree to issue a use permit if the users agree to leave the camp site in a pristine condition and solicit volunteers for the annual park cleanup day.

In Chapter 2, we describe the most common dispute resolution processes – negotiation, mediation, and court (or arbitration), with a particular focus on mediation. Chapter 2 also provides advice to disputing parties on selecting a dispute resolution process suitable for their dispute.

Reference

Ury, W. L., Brett, J. M., & Goldberg, S. B. (1993). *Getting disputes resolved*. Cambridge, MA: Program on Negotiation at Harvard Law School.

2 Dispute Resolution Processes

The primary methods of dispute resolution are negotiation (the parties or their representatives, without the intervention of a third party, seek to resolve their dispute); mediation (a third party who has no authority to impose a decision assists the parties in finding a mutually acceptable resolution of their dispute); and court or arbitration (a third party issues a binding decision determining which party wins and which loses). We discuss each of these processes below, with a focus on the approach to dispute resolution – interests, rights, or power – used in each. Then we describe mediation and explain how it can be used to recognize and respect parties' power, their rights, and their interests.

Negotiation

In dispute resolution negotiations, the parties may focus on interests, rights, or power. Not uncommonly, negotiators segue among all three approaches. Parties frequently start out with a focus on rights, as each claims it is right and the other is wrong. Since each negotiator is likely to propose a rights argument that supports its position, rights are unlikely to provide grounds for agreement. If rights-based arguments fail, negotiators may escalate to power, with one or both parties threatening to harm the other if it does not concede. If no concession is forthcoming, threats may end the negotiations. However, negotiators who realize that neither rights nor power arguments will result in a settlement of the dispute, may try interests. When parties move to interests they make an effort to focus on what each really cares about and how to integrate their different interests. Any one or the combination of these approaches may lead to agreement — or may not.

Court

Parties who are unable to resolve their dispute via negotiation often file lawsuits: "I'll see you in court!" The essence of a court proceeding is rights: lawyers for each party present evidence and arguments to the judge, who decides which party is right and so wins, and which is wrong and so loses. The culmination of a court proceeding is a judge's order directing the losing party to comply with the court's decision.

Court is the ultimate rights-based procedure. Only the parties' rights are taken into consideration in court, not their interests. As a result, the lawyer who hopes to obtain a favorable court decision must frame the client's claim as based upon a legal right. Suppose, for example, that an employee feels that he has been treated unfairly by his employer because the employer doesn't like his attitude. If there is no law or contract forbidding unfair treatment for that reason, his lawyer may reframe the claim to allege racial discrimination, which is forbidden by the law. The judge will then consider the suit on the basis of the legal terms in which it has been framed, not the sense of unfair treatment that lead to the lawsuit.

Arbitration

Arbitration follows the same basic procedure as court — presentation of evidence and arguments to a third-party decision-maker (the arbitrator). The arbitrator, like the judge, has the authority to make a binding decision determining which party is right and so wins and which party is wrong and so loses. The arbitrator's decision is not self-enforcing. If the loser does not comply voluntarily with the arbitrator's decision, the winner must go to court to obtain an order enforcing that decision. Alternatively, the loser may go to court and request that the arbitrator's decision be set aside. With rare exceptions, courts enforce arbitrators' decisions.

One major difference between court and arbitration is that the judge is chosen by the state and applies public law, while the arbitrator is chosen by the parties and applies whatever standard the parties agree will govern their dispute – most often, but not always, the terms of a contract between them. Another major difference between court and arbitration is that court proceedings are typically open to the public. Arbitration, on the other hand, is entirely private and free from public scrutiny, unless one of the parties goes to court to enforce or set aside the arbitrator's decision. Finally, although the judge is paid by the state, the arbitrator is paid by the parties. Typically each pays half the arbitrator's fee and expenses.

Arbitration is often agreed upon as a dispute resolution procedure between parties who have roughly equal bargaining power, such as unions and employers, or corporations and their suppliers. Arbitration may also be insisted upon by the more powerful party as a condition of entering into agreement with it. For example, some corporations, whose employees are not represented by a union, require their employees to arbitrate individually any disputes between them and the corporation, waiving the right to go to court.

Because of the similarity between court and arbitration as dispute resolution processes, they will for the most part be treated as one for purposes of this book.

Mediation

Mediation is negotiation with the assistance of a neutral third party – the mediator. The mediator does not have the authority to issue a binding decision, but instead helps the parties search for a mutually satisfactory resolution to their dispute. The mediator also seeks to ensure that the process takes place in an orderly manner and that the parties treat each other respectfully.

Although the standard definition of a mediator is that he/she is a third party who does not have the authority to impose a decision, some third parties, such as managers and judges, who have the authority to issue binding decisions, may set aside that authority, at least temporarily, and try to mediate. There are many reasons why they may do so. (1) They may be concerned that the relationship between the parties will suffer if one party feels that its interests have not been recognized by the third party's decision. (2) They may recognize that the disputants are likely to understand the problem far better than they do, and so arrive at an outcome that is better for both than would a third party's decision. (3) They may understand that the disputant's sense of the fairness of both the procedure and the outcome may be more positive if the disputants have participated in arriving at that outcome, as they do much more in mediation than in court or arbitration (Karambayya & Brett, 1989; Karambayya, Brett, & Lytle, 1992; Tyler, 1990).

Despite the fact that the third parties described above may choose to set aside their decisional power temporarily in favor of a mediation-like approach, the fact remains that they possess decisional power. Disputants' awareness of that fact may lead them to behave differently toward the third party than they do in the standard form of mediation in which the third party has no decisional power (Goldberg, Sander, Rogers, & Cole, 2012). In the remainder of this book, we deal solely with mediation in which the mediator has no authority to impose a settlement on disputants.

The Use of Words Indicating the Mediators's Gender

Both women and men serve as mediators, but it is awkward to write "he/she," "his/her," "she," etc., every time one refers to the mediator. Rather than use a single gender term for the mediator or the awkward "he/she," we will alternate the masculine and feminine terms, referring to the mediator as a female in some chapters, and as a male in other chapters. The gender neutral term "he/she" will occasionally be used when referring to persons other than the mediator.

There are two different approaches to mediation; one approach focuses on interests; the other on rights. (We do not address those situations in which parties go to mediation for reasons other than dispute resolution, such as seeking a better relationship. Accordingly, we do not discuss the transformative approach to mediation, which may be used in those situations.)

INTEREST-BASED OR FACILITATIVE MEDIATION

The interest-based (or facilitative) mediator seeks to help parties reach agreement by encouraging them to consider the interests — needs, concerns, fears — that underlie each of their positions. The theory underlying this approach is that even if the legal positions of disputing parties cannot be reconciled, a focus on their underlying interests may reveal a settlement possibility that neither party had considered.

The classic example of the interest-based approach to mediation is found in the story of the two men in a library who were arguing about whether the reading room window should be open or closed (Follet, 1925/1995). One man insisted it be open, the other insisted that it be closed. The librarian/mediator asked the first man why he wanted the window open, to which he responded that he wanted fresh air. She then asked the second man why he wanted the window closed. His response was that the draft coming from the open window bothered him. The librarian's solution: open the window in the next room, thus providing fresh air to the man who wanted it (his interest) and protecting the second man from the draft of an open window (his interest). Although the example is simple, experience has shown that the same basic approach can be used to settle the most complex disputes.

RIGHTS-BASED OR EVALUATIVE MEDIATION

Some mediators engage in evaluative mediation, which uses a rights-based approach. The evaluative mediator studies each party's evidence and arguments and then provides each with an evaluation of its strengths and weaknesses if the case were to go to court.

An evaluation is sometimes coupled with a prediction of the likely outcome in court, such as *"I think it highly probable that A will win at trial"* or *"I think it more likely than not that A will win at trial."* Based on that prediction, the evaluative mediator may urge the party he views as less likely to win to modify its position, and make an offer closer to the other party's position. Or, if the evaluative mediator believes that both parties have significant weaknesses (*"This case could go either way"*) he may encourage both to modify their initial positions. Ideally, the mediator's evaluation of the strengths and weaknesses of each party's case, and his prediction of the likely court outcome, will lead to a sufficient modification in the position of one or both parties to result in a settlement somewhere between their initial positions.

One shortcoming of the evaluative approach is that the party deemed by the mediator to be less likely to win in court may not accept the mediator's evaluation. It may believe that a full trial will lead to an outcome different from the mediator's prediction.

In that situation, the parties will be back where they were before the mediation began, each seeking to persuade the other that it has the stronger rights claim. Another drawback of evaluative mediation is that as a result of its focus on the legal strengths and weaknesses of each party's claim, it may fail to uncover a mutually satisfactory interest-based resolution of the dispute, one not dependent on which party is right and which is wrong.

Although many experienced mediators are capable of using a combination of both approaches, most mediators have a primary focus, and some may lack the flexibility and/or expertise to alter that focus significantly. As a result, most mediation is conducted with a central focus — interest-based or rights-based. Nonetheless, a mediator whose central focus is interests may assist the parties in evaluating their rights or power positions in order that each will have an informed view of the best outcome it can reasonably expect to attain outside mediation.

In this book, we devote most of our attention to the mediator who seeks primarily to assist the parties in resolving their dispute by focusing on their interests.

Hybrid Dispute Resolution Processes

There are many hybrid versions of these basic dispute resolution processes. Among these are med-arb, which combines mediation and arbitration; the mini-trial, which combines a simulated court trial and negotiation; the summary jury trial, which combines a simulated court trial and negotiation; parenting coordination, a form of med-arb, in which the neutral mediates between high-conflict parents, but has the authority to make decisions as an arbitrator; and early neutral evaluation, a variant of evaluative mediation. Nonetheless, negotiation, mediation, and court or arbitration remain the primary processes for dispute resolution. In the section that follows, we provide guidance to disputing parties in selecting from among these primary processes. (Suggestions for selecting from among both the primary and hybrid procedures can be found in Sander and Goldberg (1994).)

Choosing a Dispute Resolution Process

Some disputants have no choice about which dispute resolution process they will use because they have previously entered into a contract specifying the process to be used to resolve future disputes between them. Some contractual dispute resolution clauses specify a single dispute resolution process, such as arbitration. Others stipulate a series of processes, beginning with negotiation (sometimes between specified individuals), followed, if necessary, by mediation, then arbitration (see Goldberg et al., 2012, pp. 583–584, for an example of the latter).

The disadvantage of pre-dispute resolution provisions is that they may require negotiation or mediation between parties who have little or no interest in settling a particular dispute, and for whom participating in either of these processes would appear to be wasted effort. There is, however, some evidence, that mediation settlement rates are not significantly different when parties are compelled to mediate than when they choose voluntarily to do so (see Brett, Barsness, & Goldberg, 1996, pp. 262, 267; Cole, McEwen, Rogers, Coben, & Thompson, 2014–2015, § 14.16, note 7).

Additionally, some courts require parties to participate in an ADR (alternative dispute resolution) process before they can proceed to trial. Although there are many such processes, the most common ADR process to be imposed by a court is mediation. Courts may require mediation for cases ranging from small claims between consumers and businesses to lawsuits between large corporations. A mediation requirement is especially likely in family disputes in which the parents cannot agree where the children will live after the divorce and which parent will be responsible for their care.

When parties are free to choose a dispute resolution process, the first step is for each party to determine its preferred process. To do so, each party should familiarize itself with the basic processes described in the preceding pages – mediation, court, and arbitration. Next, each party should decide whether its primary goal in resolving the dispute is to be vindicated – proven to be right – or whether it seeks a settlement. If it seeks a binding determination of which party is right, only court or arbitration can provide that. If it seeks public vindication, that can be achieved only in court. If, on the other hand, a party seeks a resolution of the dispute that will focus on – and satisfy – its interests, mediation should be its choice.

REASONS FOR CHOOSING MEDIATION

Mediation is preferable to court (or arbitration) when parties seek to resolve their dispute in a comparatively inexpensive and speedy manner and to maintain control over the outcome. Mediation should also be easier on the parties' relationship than is court or arbitration, because the search for agreement does not encourage disparaging the other party in the manner that a decisional procedure may often do. In order to prevail in court or arbitration, a disputant may attack the other party in ways that will make a future relationship difficult or impossible. For example, it would not be unusual in a court proceeding to determine which parent will have custody of the children, to hear one party testify that he should prevail because "She is totally irresponsible. Here are just a few examples...." Faced with this testimony, the other spouse may testify, "He calls me irresponsible, but let me tell you what he has done." Instead of hurling accusations at each other in court, spouses who seek an agreement in mediation must persuade each other to accept terms that each can live with, a goal that is totally incompatible with disparaging each other. Mediation thus encourages future cooperation in parenting matters in a way that a third-party decision-making process is unlikely to do. For this reason, among others, mediation should always be seriously considered as the primary dispute resolution process not only in family disputes, but whenever the disputants have an interest in the quality of their relationship after the dispute has been resolved.

The cost of mediation is typically lower than that of arbitration or court because mediation does not always require legal representation. In some contexts, such as disputes between neighbors, lawyers are rarely used. Even when lawyers are used in mediation, the added expense is considerably less than in court or arbitration. Because the mediator does not make a binding decision, lawyers do not need to prepare in the way that they do for arbitration or court. For example, they may not need to engage in discovery (pre-trial collection of material from the opposing party) or prepare witnesses to testify. In addition, because the mediator is not going to make a binding decision, there is no need for the lawyers to prepare post-mediation briefs in which each recapitulates the reasons why its client should prevail.

Mediation is typically faster than court and even faster than arbitration. Civil court dockets are crowded and delays are long. Additionally, in both court and arbitration, lawyers must develop and present evidence and arguments, and, after the hearing, the judge or arbitrator must study the lawyers' presentations prior to issuing a decision. In contrast, the interest-based mediator focuses on the parties' interests, not their rights, and even the rights-based mediator need not evaluate the evidence and legal arguments with the same care as a judge because the mediator does not issue a binding decision.

To be sure, there is no guarantee of final resolution in mediation, but mediation settlement rates range up to 80%, with most mediation programs reporting settlements in 30–60% of their cases (Cole et al., 2014–2015: § 14.3, notes 16–17). Even in cases that do not settle in mediation, the mediation often clarifies parties' points of view, making a subsequent rights-based process more efficient.

It is not surprising that mediation often leads to agreement when dispute resolution negotiations have failed, since mediation addresses many of the factors that cause negotiations to fail. For example, some negotiations fail because the disputants or their representatives are too emotional to communicate without screaming insults at each other. The mediator can address this problem by placing the parties in separate rooms, so they do not communicate directly with each other, but only through the mediator. Alternatively, the mediator may set ground rules for a respectful conversation, a practice more commonly followed by family and community mediators than separating the parties. Finally, the mediator can address the negative effect of high emotion on the parties' reasoning capacity by encouraging each party to express its emotions fully, listening to each with empathy until the effect of emotion on their ability to reason has dissipated.

Another frequent cause of the failure of dispute resolution negotiations is that one or both parties do not fully understand either their own or the other disputant's interests and priorities. Returning to the Chapter 1 example of the dispute between the husband and the wife arising from his desire to buy a new car, it is unlikely that he told her that the reason he wanted a new car was to impress his friends. A mediator, however, should be able to discover the husband's interest, as well as the wife's interest in reliable transportation, and guide them to a successful resolution, such as that suggested in Chapter 1.

Still another cause for the failure of dispute resolution negotiations is the parties' differing views of the likely resolution of the dispute in court if they do not reach agreement. Sometimes the mediator can avoid addressing this difference by helping parties find an interest-based settlement that does not require a resolution of the rights issue. At other times, a mediator with evaluative skills can encourage one or both parties to alter their view of their BATNA sufficiently to lead to agreement.

> ### BATNA
>
> The term "BATNA," first used in Fisher and Ury's *Getting to Yes* (1981), is an acronym for "Best Alternative to a Negotiated Agreement." It refers to the most favorable outcome a party can reasonably anticipate if no agreement is reached in negotiation (or mediation).

Admittedly, there are situations in which none of these techniques is sufficient to bring about settlement, even among parties who prefer settlement to litigation. In general, however, the likelihood of success in mediation is sufficiently great, and its costs in time and money are sufficiently low, that it makes good sense for parties who wish to settle their dispute to try mediation before resorting to court.

NO AGREEMENT ON A DISPUTE RESOLUTION PROCESS

If the parties cannot agree on a dispute resolution process, either one party must concede to the other's choice or the dispute will be dealt with in court, the state-provided default procedure for resolving disputes. The court may, however, encourage or, pursuant to a court-adopted alternative dispute resolution program, order the parties to seek resolution in mediation or one of the nonbinding hybrid processes prior to going to trial.

We turn next, in Chapter 3, to a detailed look at the mediation process and the roles of the mediator and the parties in that process.

References

Brett, J. M., Barsness, Z. L., & Goldberg, S. B. (1996). The effectiveness of mediation: An independent analysis of cases handled by four major service providers. *Negotiation Journal, 12*, 259–269.

Cole, S. R., McEwen, C. A., Rogers, N. H., Coben, J. R., & Thompson, P. N. (2014–2015). *Mediation: Law, policy & practice (2014–2015 ed.)*. Eagan, MN: Thomson Reuters.

Fisher, R., & Ury, W. L. (1981). *Getting to yes: Negotiating agreement without giving in*. New York, NY: Houghton Mifflin Company.

Follet, M. P. (1925/1995). Constructive conflict. In P. Graham (Ed.), *Mary Parker Follett: Prophet of management* (pp. 67–87). Boston, MA: Harvard Business School Press.

Goldberg, S. B., Sander, F. E. A., Rogers, N. H., & Cole, S. R. (2012). *Dispute resolution: Negotiation, mediation, arbitration, and other processes*. New York, NY: Walters Kluwer.

Karambayya, R., & Brett, J. (1989). Managers handling disputes. *Academy of Management Journal, 32*, 687–704.

Karambayya, R., Brett, J. M., & Lytle, A. (1992). Managerial third parties: The effects of formal authority and experience on third-party roles, outcomes and perceptions of fairness. *Academy of Management Journal, 35*, 426–438.

Sander, F. E. A., & Goldberg, S. B. (1994). Fitting the forum to the fuss: A user-friendly guide to selecting an ADR procedure. *Negotiation Journal, 10*, 49–68.

Tyler, T. R. (1990). *Why people obey the law*. London: Yale University Press.

Suggested Reading

Bush, R. A. B., & Folger, J. P. (2005). *The promise of mediation* (2nd ed.). San Francisco, CA: Jossey Bass.

3 The Roles of the Mediator and the Disputing Parties at Each Step of the Mediation Process

Getting to Mediation

The first step in the mediation of a dispute is agreeing to mediate — at times a difficult step. Among the reasons disputants may be reluctant to mediate are

- doubt that mediation can succeed when the parties could not reach agreement in their negotiations;
- fear of an unfamiliar process;
- belief that one is right, so there is no need to make any of the concessions likely to be sought in mediation;
- unwillingness to meet with the other party;
- desire to be publicly vindicated as right;
- fear that the other party is not interested in settling, but rather in collecting information, and will use mediation primarily for discovery purposes;
- view that proposing mediation might be seen as a sign of weakness.

Disputants should discuss such concerns with their lawyers or others familiar with mediation.

Lawyer Representation in Mediation

Not all mediation participants are represented by lawyers. In those disputes in which the stakes – financial or other – are high, legal representation is commonplace. In those disputes in which the stakes, and/or the parties' resources, are modest, legal representation is less common. The parties may, however, be represented by someone other than a lawyer – sometimes a friend, sometimes a representative furnished by an organization (such as a union) of which the disputant is a member. Since lawyers frequently do represent the parties, we address the lawyer's role in mediation.

When disputants go to mediation without lawyers or are sent to mediation by a judge, it may be the judge or a mediation service provider who first discusses with the disputants their concerns about mediation.

Provision of Mediators by Mediation Service Firms and Courts

Mediation service firms maintain lists of qualified mediators. They also promote mediation and provide facilities for conducting mediations. If one party or its lawyer wants to mediate, but is reluctant to suggest mediation to the other party, a mediation service firm may do so. A list of mediation service providers is set out at the end of this chapter.

Courts that require parties to mediate typically maintain a list of approved mediators. Some courts allow disputants to select a mediator from the court's list; others assign mediators at random.

ADDRESSING RELUCTANCE TO MEDIATE

Whoever is engaged in proposing mediation to a reluctant party should try to understand what underlies that reluctance.

When one of the disputants doubts that mediation after an unsuccessful negotiation can lead to a settlement, the party proposing mediation should concede that the other's doubts are understandable, but explain why mediation is still worth trying:

> *Mediation is very different from negotiation and may result in a settlement even when negotiation has failed to do so. There are several reasons for this. First of all, in explaining the dispute to a mediator who knows nothing about it, each party may come to see the dispute in a different light, generating new settlement ideas. Additionally, as a result of these explanations the mediator may uncover interests that were not discussed if the negotiations focused on the parties' rights or power. The mediator may also have ideas for settlement that had not previously been discussed. Finally, the mediator may be able to discuss with each party privately and rationally its options if no settlement is reached. For all these reasons, mediation can lead to settlements when negotiations fail.*

When parties are reluctant to mediate because they have felt emotionally battered in negotiations, it should be helpful to assure them that the mediator will control the interaction. Mediators set out ground rules, for example, requiring that each party treat the other respectfully, listen without interruption, and make a genuine effort to understand — though not necessarily agree with — the other party's perspective. Mediators may separate emotional parties and serve as an empathic sounding board for their emotional venting.

Whoever is proposing mediation might, for example, address a party's reluctance to mediate like this:

Party: *I never want to see that * * * again.*

MSF (mediation service firm): *You won't have to. The mediator can put you in separate rooms and shuttle back and forth between you.*

Party: *He insults me and then we just argue with each other.*

Party's attorney: *The mediator will ensure that he does not interrupt you and she will ask the same of you. That should go a long way towards an intelligent discussion.*

When a lawyer is reluctant to recommend mediation to a client because he is unfamiliar with the mediation process, or fears appearing incompetent in mediation, a good approach is to provide the lawyer with one of the DVDs referred to at page 55 to familiarize himself with the process.

If a lawyer is reluctant to mediate because he is certain that the case is a winner in court, it may be useful to point out that one can never be certain of the outcome in court. A session with a mediator who, in addition to her focus on interests, is capable of evaluating the likelihood that his client will prevail in court might be a wise investment:

> Lawyer: *There's no point in our going to mediation. This case is a sure winner for my client.*
>
> MSF: *Can you guarantee to your client that she'll win this case?*
>
> Lawyer: *Of course not, but our chances are excellent.*
>
> MSF: *Well, the other side must not agree or they would have settled by now. Would it help move this case to resolution if the parties selected a neutral mediator who could provide both parties with a non-binding opinion as to the most likely outcome of this case in court, and see if that helps to unblock the route to settlement?*
>
> Lawyer: *That's not a bad idea. Let me raise it with my client.*

Finally, a lawyer who is reluctant to mediate because she fears that the other party's lawyer intends to use mediation as a form of discovery could be advised:

> *In the first place, discovery standards are sufficiently liberal these days that the other party can probably get all the information it wants in formal discovery, and doesn't have to use mediation for that purpose. If you are still concerned that discovery, not settlement, is the other side's motive in proposing mediation, you can protect yourself by not disclosing anything in mediation that you think they could not get in formal discovery. You should be aware, however, that doing so could*

reduce the likelihood of settlement in the mediation.
So, if you are ultimately persuaded that the other party
is after discovery, not settlement, maybe you should not
mediate.

SELECTING A MEDIATOR

Identifying potential mediators is typically the work of the parties' lawyers, unless the parties are not represented by lawyers or mediate frequently, so are familiar with potential mediators. Whoever is responsible for selecting the mediator has several options for identifying potential mediators. If one party has had a prior favorable experience with a mediator, he may propose her to the other party. Alternatively, lawyers representing the parties may contact other lawyers for recommendations or examine the lists of mediators provided by a court or local mediation service provider.

Questions to ask about a potential mediator are

- Was the mediator a good listener?
- Did the mediator treat your side fairly?
- Did the mediator treat the other side fairly?
- Did the mediator come to understand your side's interests?
- Did the mediator help you to better understand the other side's interests?
- Did the mediator involve both sides in generating options for agreement?
- Would you characterize the mediator's approach as primarily interest-based/facilitative or evaluative?
- Did the mediator provide an interpretation of the law or contract relevant to the case? (If so) did it help resolve the case?
- Do you know if the mediator has knowledge or experience in dealing with the subject matter of the case I will be mediating?
- Did your case settle?
- Would you use the same mediator again? Why? Why not?

Once the parties have a list of potential mediators, they may interview several, either separately or jointly, before selecting one.

Mediator Disclosure

If there are facts in the potential mediator's background or experience that she has not previously disclosed to the parties, and that might, if known to them, lead one or both reasonably to doubt the mediator's impartiality, those facts should be disclosed as soon as the mediator is aware that she is being considered. Examples of these include a social or professional relationship with one of the parties or their lawyers, or having served as a mediator in a prior dispute involving one of the parties (see Standard III. Conflicts of Interest, in the Model Standards of Conduct for Mediators, 2005. (http://www.americanbar.org/content/dam/aba/migrated/dispute/documents/model_standards_conduct_april2007.authcheckdam.pdf)).

It is better for the potential mediator to err on the side of too much disclosure than too little. Disclosure provides the parties maximum assistance in selecting a mediator and protects the mediator from a subsequent complaint by a party disappointed in the mediation outcome: "If we had only known what we learned after the mediation about X, we would never have selected him as the mediator."

If the lawyers cannot agree on a mutually acceptable mediator, they may authorize a third party — typically a court or one of the mediation service firms — to select the mediator. Alternatively, they may keep searching until they either agree on a mediator or abandon the idea of mediating.

Some lawyers short-circuit the search for a mutually acceptable mediator by stipulating that they will accept any mediator selected by the other party, subject to the requirement that the mediator satisfy certain criteria of competence. Those criteria are often satisfied by the mediator's name appearing on the list of mediators approved by a court or by a mediation service firm. This is not as risky as it might appear because the mediator has no decision-making authority. If you allow the other side to select the mediator with whom he is comfortable, it may be easier to reach a mutually acceptable agreement.

MEDIATOR FEES

Mediators typically set their own fees; most often they are paid on an hourly or daily basis. Some mediators charge a cancellation fee if a scheduled mediation day is canceled. The mediator's fee will rarely be negotiated by the parties. The parties may, however, decline to use a particular mediator if they view the mediator's fee to be excessive. The amount of the mediator's fee is likely to vary according to the complexity of the dispute and the availability of mediators with the experience and expertise required by the type of dispute. Most often, each party will pay an equal share of the mediator's fee (see Chapter 5 for ethical issues when shares are unequal). If the mediation takes place under the auspices of a court, the mediator's services may be provided without cost to the parties or at a fee set by the court. Some family mediators offer sliding fees based on the income of the parties. Additionally, there are some not-for-profit organizations that provide mediation free of charge.

CHOOSING A PLACE AND TIME TO MEDIATE

The parties will need to decide where the mediation will take place and approximately how much time they should schedule for the mediation. Sometimes mediation takes place on the premises of one of the parties or in the office of one of their lawyers. If the parties are too hostile to meet in either of these locations, they may select a neutral location, such as a hotel, a church, a restaurant private dining room, the offices of a lawyer not involved in the dispute, or the offices of a mediation service firm. Ideally, the location selected for the mediation will have a conference room large enough to accommodate all participants in the joint meetings, as well as break-out rooms where the parties can meet for separate strategy sessions and the mediator can meet separately with each party.

Determining how much time to allot for mediation is difficult because one never knows how long it will take to reach agreement or determine that no agreement is possible. The more complex the issues and the more bitter the conflict, the more time may be needed for the mediation, at times several days spread out over as many months. Family mediations usually require sessions spread over several weeks, but these sessions typically take only an hour or two, not all day. Small claims and landlord—tenant mediations also last only an hour or two, and are usually concluded in one session — often on the same day the parties appear in court, and the judge suggests that they mediate rather proceed to a court trial.

PRE-MEDIATION DISCUSSIONS
Pre-Mediation Briefs
In a complex or high-stakes mediation, parties or their attorneys may meet with the mediator, either by telephone or in person prior to the first mediation session. One issue typically dealt with in such meetings is whether the parties will submit pre-mediation written presentations ("briefs") setting out the facts and arguments of the parties, as well as any current settlement proposals. Such briefs are sometimes submitted solely to the mediator, sometimes to the mediator with a copy for the other party.

Pre-mediation briefs have advantages and disadvantages. They educate the mediator and ensure that the parties (or at least their representatives) are prepared when they arrive at the mediation, but they also increase the cost of mediation. There is also the risk that in the course of preparing a brief, the party's representative will convince herself that the party she represents is right, and so be less amenable to an interest-based search for a mutually acceptable resolution of the dispute.

Written Agreements
The parties should also decide prior to the mediation whether any agreement reached at mediation should be written, at least in outline form — known as a "term sheet" — and signed before the parties leave the mediation site. Alternatively, any agreement reached at mediation may be regarded as tentative, allowing each party a limited time after the mediation to accept or reject that agreement. The advantage of having a written and signed term sheet before the parties leave the mediation is that it ensures that the agreement reached at mediation is not undone by second thoughts a party may have after the mediation. It also protects the agreement from second-guessing by those who were not at the mediation and lack a full understanding of the discussions that led to the agreement.

The advantage of not requiring a signed term sheet as soon as agreement is reached is that it allows the parties to reflect calmly, away from the pressures of mediation, on whether the tentative agreement serves their interests. Arguably, if one or both of the parties concludes that the tentative agreement is unwise, it is better to know that before rather than after attempting to carry out the agreement. Conversely, if both parties, on reflection, support the tentative agreement, they may be more fully committed to its implementation than if they had no time to reflect.

Pre-Dispute Mediation Agreements and the Parties' Ability to Determine Mediation Procedures at the Time of Mediation

This discussion of whether or not to agree to pre-mediation briefs and written agreements immediately after agreement has been reached assumes that the parties are free to make those decisions. That may not be the case if they have a contractual agreement to mediate, or they are mediating because of court requirements. In these cases, procedural decisions such as those described above may be predetermined.

Joint Meeting or Separate Meetings to Begin the Mediation

Whether the mediation is to begin with a meeting of both parties and the mediator (joint meeting), or with separate meetings between the mediator and each of the parties (caucuses) is a common subject of pre-mediation discussions. Alternatively, it may be discussed when the parties meet to begin the mediation, but before they have begun discussions aimed at resolving the dispute.

Those who support beginning the mediation with a joint meeting assert that:

- The mediator will have the opportunity to explain the procedures and rules of mediation to all participants at the same time, thus reducing the risk of different understandings.
- Each party will have an opportunity to express itself in the presence of the other — not only about the facts of the dispute, but also the outcome it seeks and the reasons it should obtain that outcome. Particularly if all or most pre-mediation discussions of the dispute have taken place between the parties' representatives, a joint meeting may bring to light a different understanding of the dispute. At times this different

understanding may of lead one party to say, "If I had known that was all you wanted, we could have resolved this matter long ago."

- Each party will have the opportunity to express its emotions (such as disappointment or anger) to the other party, which may lead to a reduction in the strength of those emotions, permitting the mediation to proceed on a more reasoned basis.
- The mediator who has the opportunity to observe the interaction of the disputants in a joint meeting may gather useful settlement clues. For example, the mediator's preliminary meetings with the parties' representatives may have led her to believe that a particular issue is of great importance to both parties, and that neither will easily concede on that issue. If, however, at an initial joint meeting, one party's expression of the importance of that issue to it stirs little reaction from the other party, the mediator may infer that the issue is of major importance to only one party. Such information may provide the basis for a trade that will be a step on the way to resolution.

Those who support beginning the mediation in separate sessions believe that a joint session, rather than leading to a reduction in the emotional barriers to resolution, is likely to increase those barriers as each party expresses its anger toward the other in the presence of the latter. The proponents of beginning in separate session also assert that:

- Initial separate sessions in which the mediator focuses on building an empathic relationship with each disputant can reduce the likelihood that parties will arrive at the joint session angry at the other disputant and defensive toward the mediator.
- Initial separate sessions should emphasize understanding the emotional landscape of the dispute, rather than the substantive issues presented (Swaab, R.I., & Brett, J.M. (Working paper.)).

The mediator may wish to suggest to the parties that they start with joint or separate sessions depending on what order of working with the parties she thinks will be most effective under the circumstances.

Beginning the Mediation

Regardless of whether the mediation begins in joint or separate session, the mediator should explain her role, confirm that all persons necessary to resolve the dispute are present or can be contacted during the mediation, and set out the rules and procedures that will be followed.

THE MEDIATOR'S ROLE

The mediator should make clear that she is neither a judge nor an arbitrator, but rather a neutral who will help the parties try to find a mutually acceptable resolution of their dispute. Deciding whether or not a particular settlement is acceptable is, however, up to each party, and the mediator should not exert pressure on either party to accept a particular settlement or, indeed, to accept any settlement at all.

Keys to Mediator Success

Recent research (Goldberg & Shaw, 2007; Goldberg, Shaw, & Brett, 2009), in which approximately 500 representatives (mostly lawyers) of mediating parties assessed the reasons for mediator success in assisting parties to resolve disputes, found that the most frequently cited attribute of a successful mediator was the mediator's ability to gain the trust and confidence of the disputing parties. Mediators were said to achieve this by one or more of the following behaviors:

- being friendly, empathic, respectful, caring;
- demonstrating high integrity through honesty, neutrality, fairness, respecting confidentiality;
- being smart, well-prepared, understanding the issues

The mediator who wishes to succeed in aiding the parties to reach agreement should demonstrate these behaviors from the very beginning of the mediation. For example, in explaining her role in the mediation process, as well as in explaining mediation rules and procedures, the mediator should convey the sense that she is confident and skilled in the mediation process. In doing so, the mediator encourages trust in both the process and herself.

INTRODUCTION OF THOSE PRESENT

If the mediation begins in joint session, the mediator should ask each person in the room to introduce himself/herself. Most of those present may be known to each other, but not to everybody, and it can be disconcerting to have someone present on behalf of one party who is not known to the other party.

Avoiding the Appearance of Bias

If the mediator is acquainted with one of the parties or its lawyer, either professionally or socially, it is important that the mediator show no sign of favoritism toward that person. She should, for example, avoid greeting that person with more warmth than she greets others, or addressing only that person, and no one else, by his/her first name. Parties to a dispute are often extraordinarily sensitive to any signs of favoritism by the mediator, and the mediator should be vigilant to avoid any words or actions that might be interpreted as demonstrating favoritism.

ENSURING THE ATTENDANCE (OR AVAILABILITY) OF ALL NECESSARY PARTIES

The parties should ensure that all persons necessary to discuss and resolve the dispute are present at the mediation, and the mediator should confirm their presence. If someone whose approval will be necessary for a final resolution is not present, the parties and the mediator should ensure that he/she can be easily contacted to discuss a potential settlement. This solution is less desirable, however, than having all decision-makers present at the mediation. A person who was not present as a potential settlement was discussed and developed may have difficulty in appreciating the reasons that led the parties to agree to that settlement.

RULES OF MEDIATION

It is important that the mediator begin by setting out the rules of mediation. Among the most important rules are the following.

Respect

A central rule of mediation is that all participants are entitled to be treated with respect. This means that each participant will be

given the opportunity to speak, and that there will be no interruptions of a speaker.

Rules of Evidence

The mediator may also want to note, either at the beginning of
the mediation, or when the issue arises, that the rules of evidence
that apply in court do not apply in mediation. This caution is
appropriate even if neither party is represented by a lawyer, since
a nonrepresented party may want to act like a lawyer, raising
objections to what is said by the other party. The mediator
should make clear that no objections to a participant's remarks
will be allowed on grounds such as lack of relevance or
materiality.

The reason for this rule is that the goal of mediation is not to
resolve legal issues, but to assist the parties in resolving their dispute. Since a resolution in mediation may be affected by an issue
that is not relevant or material to legal issues, rules of evidence
developed to deal with legal issues have no place in mediation.
For example, in a dispute between neighbors about whether one
of them is playing music too loudly, in violation of a municipal
noise law, the alleged violator may say of the complaining party,
"She doesn't respect me." While legally irrelevant to whether the
noise law has been violated, the mediator may discover that
the reason one neighbor has continued to play music loudly is
that she thinks the complaining neighbor has not addressed her
respectfully when asking that the music volume be reduced.
Enabling the complaining neighbor to understand that her
complaints will be heeded if she makes them respectfully may
be sufficient to resolve the dispute and restore calm to the
neighborhood.

Commitment

After the mediator has set out the rules and answered the parties'
questions about the process, the mediator may ask the parties to
make an oral (or even written) pledge to abide by the rules of
mediation. Doing so should lead to a greater commitment to
follow the rules than would sitting by silently while the rules are
explained. If necessary, the mediator can use this commitment to
enforce the rules. (*Mister X* (who has just interrupted the other
party), *I thought you told me you were going to abide by the no
interruptions rule.*) Such a gentle reminder is usually effective in
obtaining compliance.

Voluntary Nature of Mediation

Normally the parties are as free to leave mediation when they wish as they are to decline to mediate in the first place. At times however, the parties are in mediation because of a contractual agreement to mediate or a court order to do so. Such an agreement or order may require them to remain in mediation for a specified time.

Searching for a Mutually Acceptable Resolution of the Dispute

OPENING STATEMENTS

When the parties meet in joint session, whether at the opening of the mediation, or after initial separate sessions, each party or its representative will typically make an opening statement that sets out that party's position, the facts as it views them, and the reasons why, on the basis of those facts, it is right under the law, relevant contract terms, or principles of fairness, and should receive whatever it claims from the other party — money, property, child custody, etc.

MOVING FROM POSITIONS TO INTERESTS

After the opening statements, the parties and the mediator are ready to begin the search for a mutually acceptable resolution of the dispute. In interest-based mediation, the mediator's role in this search consists of assisting each party to (1) understand its own and the other party's interests and priorities; (2) develop potential settlements; (3) make the best settlement offers possible, consistent with its interests and priorities; (4) compare the best agreement available in mediation with the best outcome it can reasonably expect outside mediation (BATNA). In carrying out these tasks, the mediator's goal is to assist each party in determining if the best agreement available in mediation is better than its BATNA.

TECHNIQUES FOR IDENTIFYING INTERESTS AND PRIORITIES

Defining and Ordering Issues

After the parties' opening statements, the mediator, preferably in joint session, should summarize her understanding of the issues, ask the parties to confirm her understanding, and determine if there are other issues that need to be addressed. (The mediator wants to be certain that there will be no surprise issues that pop up at the end of the mediation and upset a settlement arrived at on all the previously stated issues.)

Next, the mediator should encourage the parties to discuss the issues, explaining their concerns. She may use this discussion to identify issues on which the parties are not too far apart, so might be resolved promptly, thus providing momentum toward settlement. Alternatively, she may conclude from this discussion that there are one or two key issues that must be resolved before progress can be made toward an overall settlement. In either event, she may establish the ground rule that no agreement on a single issue is final until all issues are resolved. ("Nothing is final until everything is final.") By doing so, she encourages the parties to reach tentative agreements on individual issues while still maintaining the flexibility to alter those tentative agreements if necessary to reach overall agreement.

When the discussion appears to have exhausted the potential for agreement in joint session, most mediators will suggest that the mediation continue in separate sessions.

Separate Sessions as Means of Encouraging the Parties to Share All Relevant Information with the Mediator

Separate meetings with each disputant and its representative are of great value in the search for a resolution of the dispute. Such meetings may enable a party to vent emotions that, if expressed in the presence of the other party, might lead to an abrupt termination of the mediation. Such sessions may also encourage a disputant to reveal confidential information that it has not been willing to reveal to the other party — the facts as it sees them, its interests (needs, concerns, fears), and its views concerning an acceptable resolution of the dispute. If both parties make such disclosures to the mediator in their separate sessions, the mediator should have more information than either party, and should be in a better position than either party to lead the negotiation to a mutually satisfactory result. Furthermore, such a mutually satisfactory result can be achieved without the mediator disclosing to either party the confidential information it has learned from the other.

An example of a mediator using confidential information obtained in a separate session to assist the parties in reaching settlement, without disclosing what she learned in the separate sessions, might be this:

> Mediator (in separate session with Party A): *You just told me that a major part of the reason that you are suing Party B for the money you say he owes you under the contract is that your business has recently been struggling and you need that money to keep afloat. Is that right?*

> Party A: *Yes, but you can't tell him that.*

> Mediator: OK, *but if he will pay you 75% of the amount you claim – and do it immediately so that you can get your business back on track – would you accept that as a satisfactory resolution of this matter?*

> Party A: *Well, I wouldn't be happy about it because he owes me all of my claim, but since it will get me back on my feet, I'll accept it – if he'll pay in the next 30 days.*

> Mediator (in separate session with Party B): *You've told me that you think A's claim is wildly inflated, but let me ask you this. If you could resolve this matter today, and avoid any more lawyer's bills, would you be willing to pay 75% of his claim?*

> Party B: *Not happily, but I'd do it.*

> Mediator: OK, *let me see what A says to that. By the way, how soon could you make payment?*

> Party B: *The sooner this is done, the happier I'll be. How about 15 days?*

> Mediator: *Let me see what he says.*

Mediator Guidelines for Conducting Separate Sessions

If the mediator intends to meet separately with the parties, the guarantee of confidentiality concerning what is said in such meetings should be communicated to them at the start of the mediation and repeated prior to any separate sessions with each of the parties. The mediator might also, if she senses that that a party is considering making a disclosure, but is hesitant to do so, say something like *You don't have to be nervous about telling me what's on your mind. You have my commitment that I won't disclose to the other party anything you say without your consent ... and if I didn't live up to that commitment*

I wouldn't last long as a mediator. (Limitations on the mediator's ability to guarantee the confidentiality of what she has learned in a separate session are discussed in Chapter 5, pages 81–85.)

Parties may be concerned that during a separate session the other party will make statements to the mediator that are not true, but that cannot be challenged by the party not in the separate session because he/she does not know about them. The mediator should acknowledge this concern if it arises, but point out to the parties that if one party, during a separate meeting, makes a settlement proposal to the mediator that is based on inaccurate information, and the mediator presents that settlement proposal to the other party, it can and should reject that proposal. Ultimately, the parties' protection against a settlement based on false statements made by the other party during a separate session lies in their power to reject any proposed settlement which does not satisfy their interests.

If the mediator meets separately with one party, she should also meet separately with the other party, if for no other reason than to avoid an appearance of partiality. It is not necessary that the time spent in separate sessions with one party be the same as with the other, but if a separate session with one party takes considerably longer than preceding sessions with the other party, the mediator, also in order to avoid an appearance of partiality, should provide the latter with an explanation for the extra time. *I'm sorry that my meeting with X is taking/took so long, but they are discussing some key issues* or … *but they are collecting information that they thought might be helpful in moving us toward settlement.*

Another approach to separate sessions is for the mediator to arrange private meetings between selected individuals from each party. The most common such meetings involve the mediator and a representative of each party, either separately or together. These meetings are often used to discuss sensitive issues (including potential settlements) in a small group to test out their receptivity before raising them with all the participants.

A mediator may conclude that a private meeting between certain individuals from each party may be the key to resolution. For example, if technical issues are involved, such as whether a company's proposed staffing of a manufacturing operation is feasible, a settlement might be achieved by putting together one or two technicians from each side (Company and Union) who best understand the details of the operation. As technicians who share common knowledge, they may be able to discuss and resolve technical issues without partisan wrangling. Another example is that in some cases of employee discipline, the company, before agreeing to reduce or eliminate the discipline, may need assurance that the disciplined employee will act appropriately in the future. A private meeting between the disciplined employee and his/her supervisor may achieve that result. It also may lead to a joint sense of ownership of the solution, and a mutual commitment to make it work. (Such meetings should not be conducted without the consent of the parties.)

No Separate Sessions

Some mediators reject the use of separate sessions (Friedman & Himmelstein, 2008), not because they are ineffective in facilitating a mutually acceptable resolution of the dispute, but because such resolutions place the mediator, rather than the parties, at the center of the dispute resolution process. They view this as contrary to the core mediation philosophy of facilitating resolution by the parties, whose dispute it is, rather than the lawyers or the mediator.

Mediators taking this perspective also argue that if the settlement is the result of the mediator going back and forth between the parties, collecting information about interests and priorities from each, it will be the mediator who is the architect of the settlement, not the parties. As a result, the parties may lack sufficient familiarity with the settlement to implement it successfully. Furthermore, they assert that if the dispute was resolved as a result of the mediator meeting separately with each party, the parties will not have learned as much as they otherwise might have about negotiating and resolving disputes directly with each other. These concerns are particularly relevant when the parties have a continuing relationship, such as that of divorcing parents with children, a company and a union, or parties united by a long-term contract.

In deciding whether or not to use separate sessions, the mediator will weigh these concerns against the advantages of separate sessions in reaching agreement.

Other Mediator Techniques for Encouraging Disclosure of Interests and Priorities

Asking well-crafted questions, listening carefully to the responses, and sometimes reformulating those responses can be useful in uncovering interests and priorities. These techniques are particularly valuable if used in separate meetings in which the participants do not fear that their answers to the questions or their responses to reformulations may be used against them by the other party. Accordingly, we assume in what follows that the mediator is meeting separately with the parties.

Questioning. Questioning by the mediator, as long as it is not viewed by the parties as interrogation, may be a useful means of learning about their interests and priorities. The mediator's tone of voice is of great importance in this respect. An aggressive tone of voice, or one that suggests that the party being questioned is in the wrong, can easily alter or even cut off that party's responses. Questions should be asked in a neutral tone that suggests genuine curiosity, empathy, and a real desire to understand the party's perspective.

Unfortunately, asking a party directly, "What are the interests underlying your position in this matter?" may not elicit useful information. Mediation participants have typically not been trained to understand the difference between positions and interests, and are likely to respond to the above question with either a blank stare or by restating their position. As a result, the mediator may need to rely on indirect questioning to learn each party's interests and priorities.

Some useful questions:

- *What, if anything, should I know that didn't come out in the joint session when we were all together?* This question is typically asked at the beginning of the first separate session with each party. If something was not disclosed in the joint session, it may be because it was regarded by the nondisclosing party as both important and sensitive. For example, an RV owners group protesting a government agency's denial of a permit for an overnight stay in a public park (see Chapter 1) may be suffering from declining membership, and so need to obtain concessions from the agency to demonstrate to its members that they should continue to pay dues. This interest, as important as it is to the RV group, is unlikely to be raised in the joint session with the agency.

- *Has the other side made a settlement proposal?* [If so] *Why did you reject that proposal?* The key word in the latter question is "why." A disputant may be unable to articulate his/her interests, but a mediator who continually (but gently) challenges the disputant's conclusory assertions by asking "Why?" or "Why do you say that?" should succeed in finding those interests.

A variant of the same technique is for the mediator to present two settlement proposals, similar in all but one or two respects. In indicating which of the two proposals is preferable and explaining why, a party will reveal her interests. Suppose, for example, that after the first year of a 2-year lease a landlord evicted a tenant because the tenant's dog was allegedly barking at night and disturbing other tenants. The evicted tenant filed a complaint in Housing Court, and 6 months after the eviction, the matter was referred to the City Mediation Center. After some back and forth between the mediator and the two parties, the mediator learned from the landlord that other tenants' dogs bark considerably more at night than did the evicted tenant's dog, so that the case for eviction is not very strong. The mediator also learned from the tenant that he would rather move elsewhere than return to the apartment from which he was evicted. However, the only alternative rental he had been able to find in the 6 months since he was evicted cost 25% more than what he had been paying. The mediator next went to the landlord:

> Mediator: *I've talked to your former tenant and I have two possible settlement ideas. I don't know if either would be acceptable to him, but I wanted to talk to you first. One idea would be to put him back in the apartment for the six months remaining on his lease, but with no compensation for the time after he was evicted and had to pay a higher rent elsewhere. Another idea would be to terminate the lease now. To get him to accept that, though, you'd probably have to pay him the difference between his rent here and the greater amount he has had to pay for the last six months and will probably have to pay for the next six months. Which of those settlements would be less painful for you?*

> Landlord: *I don't like either and I certainly don't want to hand over any money to that SOB, but it would be even*

*worse to have him back here. I want to terminate the
lease and get him out of here.*

The mediator now knows that the landlord's primary interest
is keeping the former tenant out of the building and that the
tenant, too, would prefer to live elsewhere. This should lead
the mediator to focus her efforts on a resolution under which the
landlord will pay a sum the tenant will regard as sufficient to
rent elsewhere.

Active Listening. The mediator who wants to maximize the
value of her questions also needs to engage in active listening.
This technique requires that the mediator:

- Allow the speaker to express himself fully, not cutting him
  off.
- Listen with total attention to what is said.
- Express no opinion (other than interest) about what is said.
- Show that she has been listening attentively by restating what
  has been said.
- Show empathy (an understanding and appreciation of the
  speaker's experiences or feelings), but not sympathy (a sharing of the speaker's experiences or feelings). *That must have
  been really hard for you* (empathy), not *I feel sorry for the
  hardships you have been through* (sympathy). An expression
  of empathy is relatively neutral; an expression of sympathy
  implies support, which is inconsistent with the mediator's
  duty of neutrality.

Listening and reacting in this fashion demonstrates the
mediator's genuine interest and concern in what is being said.
It encourages full responses to the mediator's questions, and aids
the mediator in discerning the speaker's interests and priorities.
Active listening also increases the parties' confidence and trust in
the mediator as someone who genuinely cares about them.

One Mediator's Experience

The first time I mediated a complex commercial dispute,
I was terrified. The parties were represented by sophisti-
cated lawyers with a firm grasp of the relevant law and
extensive knowledge of each party's business. If they could
not find a mutually acceptable resolution, how could I, who

had neither the specialized legal knowledge of the lawyers nor their familiarity with the parties' businesses? The answer, I discovered, lay in asking lots of questions and listening carefully to the answers. I learned that if I listened sufficiently carefully to what each party said, they would, often unwittingly, tell me what type of settlement they would accept.

Reformulation. Still another means by which the mediator can discern the interests and priorities of the parties is by reformulating what they say. There are different types of reformulation, each of which serves a slightly different mediator goal.

The purpose of *echo or mirror reformulation* is to demonstrate to the speaker that the mediator has been listening attentively and understands what has been said. This encourages the speaker to continue speaking and protects against mediator misunderstanding. The mediator engaged in mirror/echo reformulation will typically ask the speaker to confirm her reformulation:

Mediator: *From your point of view, your neighbors playing music late at night is unfair to someone like you who has to go to work in the morning. Do I have it right?*

Party: *Yes; that's why I went to the police station to file a complaint.*

A mediator may learn more about a party's interests by reformulating *feelings*. For example:

Mediator: *It seems to me that you were even more upset at your neighbors' response to your complaints about their late night music than you were at the music itself. Is that accurate?*

Party: *No; that was just them being impolite. I didn't like it, but I can live with it. It's their keeping me from sleeping by playing that disgusting music all night that is really interfering with my ability to get to work on time.*

Positive reformulation consists of restating in a positive manner what has been stated negatively. If the reformulation is successful in changing the tone of the discussion, it may be an important step to resolution:

> Party: *It's their playing that disgusting rap music all night that is really interfering with my ability to get to work on time.*
>
> Mediator: *So a change in their behavior that would enable you to get a good night's sleep and get to work on time is what you are after, right?*
>
> Party: *Right ... and that's something they just don't understand.*

In a *synthesis reformulation*, the mediator focuses on the essential elements of what has been said. The mediator may use a synthesis reformulation to move the mediation toward settlement:

> Mediator: *If I understand correctly, your neighbors are playing loud music late at night and that interferes with your ability to get a good night's sleep and get to work on time the next day. Is that right?*
>
> Party: *Yes*
>
> Mediator: *And getting to work on time is important to you. Right?*
>
> Party: *Yes*
>
> Mediator: *Are there nights when their playing music would not interfere so much with your ability to go to work the next day? Are weekends different from weekdays?*
>
> Party: *Sure. I don't work Saturday or Sunday. So if they would agree not to play music loudly after say 10:00 p.m. except on Friday and Saturday nights that would be a big help. I could always sleep at my sister's house on the week-end.*
>
> Mediator: *If they would agree to that, would you withdraw your complaint?*
>
> Party: *Absolutely.*
>
> Mediator: *OK; I'd like you to present that idea to them, and I'll coach you on the best way to do so.*

The Case of the Travelling Mechanic

Many of the techniques used by mediators to assist disputing parties in reaching a mutually satisfactory agreement can be found in the Case of the Travelling Mechanic, which is drawn from an actual mediation of a dispute between a discharged employee and his former employer.

The mediator learned in the opening joint session that the employee had been terminated from his job as a travelling mechanic (one who travels from one employer facility to another to maintain and repair machinery) because of his numerous accidents while driving a company truck. According to investigations by the company safety committee, each of these accidents was due to the employee's careless driving. The company also learned from the state's Department of Motor Vehicles that the employee had five convictions in the last 3 years for speeding in his personal vehicle.

The employee argued that the termination was not for good cause (the contractual requirement for termination) because the accidents were not due to his negligence. He sought reinstatement to his job and compensation for all lost pay and benefits.

Prior to the mediation, the company offered to pay the employee 6 months' pay (the employee was terminated a year ago) in full and final settlement of his claim.

Here is the mediator in her first separate meeting with the employee.

Mediator: *What should I know that didn't come out in the joint session, when we were all together?*

Employee: *Only that the company doesn't have the vaguest idea of what it's like to have to live without pay for a year.*

Mediator: *I can certainly understand how difficult that must be.* (The mediator demonstrates empathy.) *Has the company made a settlement offer?*

Employee: *If you can call it that. I've been out of work for a year, and they offered me just six months' pay to settle my claim.*

Mediator: *Why didn't you accept the offer?* (Asking the reason for the employee's position is intended to focus the discussion on the employee's interests.)

Employee: *Because I want my job back, not some money to make me go away.*

Mediator: *So if I understand you correctly, a settlement in which you receive half your lost pay is not acceptable. Do I have it right?*

Employee: *Yes*

Mediator: *If the employer offered 100% of your lost pay, would you accept that offer?*

Employee: *No.*

Mediator: *Why not?*

Employee: *Because I want to keep working.*

Mediator: *Why is that so important to you?*

Employee: *Because I'm 50 years old and if this employer fires me I'll never get another job.*

Mediator: *So the most important issue for you is getting your job back. Is that right?* [The mediator confirms the employee's primary interest.]

Employee: *Absolutely*!

Mediator: *Is it OK with you if I tell the employer that the most important issue for you is getting your job back?* (Consistent with her pre-caucus commitment, the mediator asks the employee's permission before sharing with the employer what she has learned in the separate session with the employee about the employee's primary interest.)

Employee: *Yes.*

Mediator: *OK, let me talk to the employer and see what they will offer.*

As a result of her questioning, the mediator has learned that the employee's primary interest is reinstatement to his prior job. The employee is also interested in receiving compensation for the period he has been out of work, but his first priority is reinstatement. Armed with this information, the mediator will next meet separately with the employer to determine its interests.

After having repeated her assurances of confidentiality, the mediator begins her questioning, as she did with the employee, asking, *What, if anything, should I know that didn't come out in the joint session?* If that question turns up anything of interest, the mediator will follow up on it. Otherwise, she is likely to turn to the employer's pre-mediation settlement offer. (Settlement offers that have been rejected provide fertile ground for uncovering interests and priorities. The terms of the offer provide insight into what is more and less important for the party making the offer; the reasons for rejection provide similar insight into the other party's interests and priorities).

> Mediator: *According to the employee, you offered to set-tle this matter by paying him 50% of his lost pay. Is that accurate?* (The mediator wants to be certain that what she was told by the employee about the terms of the offer was accurate.)
>
> Employer: *Yes, but he turned it down.*
>
> Mediator: *Do you know why he turned it down?*
>
> Employer: *No; he just said that it was a pile of crap not worth discussing. That upset me. . . Who does he think he is telling me that my offering to pay him for six months when he hasn't been working for me is a piece of crap?*
>
> Mediator: *So you think your offer was reasonable?* (A positive restatement by the mediator.)
>
> Employer: *I certainly do!*
>
> Mediator: *Well, if you made a reasonable financial offer that he turned down, what do you think it will take to get this matter resolved?*
>
> Employer: *More money perhaps?*
>
> Mediator: *Well, he told me that his primary interest is getting reinstated to his job, and getting more money won't do that ... Would you consider rehiring him?* (The mediator shares the employee's primary interest in an effort to encourage the employer to make a settlement offer that would satisfy that interest.)
>
> Employer: *Not in a million years!*
>
> Mediator: *Why not? Has he been an unsatisfactory employee?* (Once again, asking the "why" question encourages the disclosure of underlying interests.)

Employer: *No, he's a good mechanic. But, he's had three accidents in company trucks. The last one cost us $150,000 because he totaled someone's car with injuries to the driver. He's also had five speeding convictions in the last three years in his personal vehicle. He's a hazard on the road and there's no way we'll put him back behind the wheel of a company truck. The risk to the company is just too great. We'd increase our back pay offer to 100% of his lost pay, but that's as far as we'd go.*

Mediator: *I thought you might say that, so the last time I talked to the employee I asked if he would settle this matter for 100% of his back pay, but no reinstatement. Without hesitating, he said "no," that what he wanted was reinstatement.*

Employer: *Well then, we're at an impasse because we don't want him back driving a company truck.*

Mediator: *Can I tell him that, as well as your reasons?* (The mediator seeks permission to share the company's interests with the employee.)

Employer: *He should know by now, but you can certainly tell him.*

Mediator: *Here's what I suggest. While I talk to the employee, you talk among yourselves and see if you can come up with a settlement suggestion that we haven't talked about yet, but that you could accept and that you think he should also accept. I will ask the employee to do the same. Is that OK?*

Employer: *Sure, we'll try.*

Encouraging Realistic Settlement Proposals: Coaching the Parties

The mediator's last admonition to the employer — that it should make a settlement proposal that it would accept *and that the employee should also accept* — is intended both to encourage an acceptable settlement proposal and, equally important, to discourage an unrealistic settlement proposal that could offend the other party. Even early in the mediation, when the parties are exchanging proposals intended to signal their firmness on certain issues, rather than with any realistic expectation that those proposals will be accepted, the mediator should discourage proposals that may offend the other party by their extreme nature – a monetary demand, for example, that far exceeds anything the parties have previously discussed. The mediator cannot forbid a party from making such an offer. She may, however, point out that the other party is likely to take it as a sign that the party who made it has no genuine interest in settlement. This risks creating a chilling effect on the discussions and perhaps dooming the mediation.

The mediator who discourages unrealistic settlement proposals for fear that they will scuttle the mediation is actually engaged in coaching the parties in sound negotiating behavior. Another example of mediator coaching is when a mediator discourages one of the parties from attacking the personal integrity of the other during a joint session. Some mediators shy away from coaching for fear it will be viewed as improper assistance to one of the parties. Other mediators believe that as long as their coaching suggestions are designed to lead to settlement, not to influence the terms of the settlement, coaching is consistent with the mediator's duty of neutrality.

Developing Potential Settlements

SEEKING CREATIVE PROPOSALS FROM THE PARTIES

The parties know each other and their situation better than does the mediator. If she restates their dispute in terms of their interests rather than their positions, they might have useful settlement ideas.

> Mediator (to Employer): *Have you come up with any settlement ideas since we last talked?*

> Employer: *No; we still don't want him behind the wheel of one of our trucks.*

> Mediator: *OK, I understand that you have a strong interest in protecting the company from liability arising from*

his driving. But you also told me that he's a good mechanic, and you certainly have an interest in having good mechanics on the payroll. Is there any way you could reinstate him as a mechanic without him driving a company truck?

Employer (after a brief internal discussion): *Well, if you put it that way, we do have positions for stationary mechanics, who do not drive, but stay in one location. We could reinstate him to one of those positions, but he'd have to understand that he'll never drive a company truck again.*

Mediator: *OK, let me run that by him and see what his response is.*

WORKING WITH THE PARTIES' PROPOSALS

If one of the parties makes a settlement proposal that is not wholly unreasonable, but is unacceptable to the other party, the mediator should ask the latter, <u>Why</u> *is their proposal not acceptable?* Not uncommonly, the mediator can use the response to that question to encourage a proposal that will be acceptable. For example, in the case of the travelling mechanic, the following discussion might take place:

Mediator (to Employee): *The Company has offered to reinstate you as a stationary mechanic, but not as a travelling mechanic, because they don't want you driving a company truck. Is that an acceptable resolution of this matter?*

Employee: *No.*

Mediator: *Why not? Is there any difference in the work of the travelling mechanic and the stationary mechanic?*

Employee: *No; they both do repair and maintenance work on company machinery. But the traveling mechanic gets paid more and I don't see why I should take a pay cut because of a trumped-up charge of negligent driving.*

Mediator: *If lower pay, not different work, is your reason for not going back as a stationary mechanic, does that give you any ideas for an acceptable settlement?*

Employee: *Sure. If the company would hire me as a stationary mechanic, but pay me at the traveling mechanic rate, I'd take that … if they'd also reimburse me for all the pay I've lost while being out of work.*

Mediator: *OK, I'll pass that idea on and let's see what they say.*

DIFFERENT TYPES OF AGREEMENT

Although proposed agreements that rest upon the parties' interests and priorities have the greatest chance of being acceptable, the experienced mediator knows that certain types of agreement are capable of satisfying interests that are common barriers to settlement.

Agreements of Limited Duration

At times, parties can envision a settlement that satisfies their immediate concerns, but one or both is reluctant to enter into that settlement for fear that it might give rise to future problems. In this situation, the mediator may suggest an agreement of limited duration, so that the immediate problem can be resolved and future problems dealt with when and if they arise. Thus, the employer in the travelling mechanic case might agree to reinstate the employee to his prior job for a period of 3 months, with that period to be extended if the company is satisfied with his performance over that time. If not, the parties will reopen negotiations.

Contingent Agreements

Another way to deal with uncertainty about the future is by an agreement that explicitly addresses the occurrence of an uncertain event. In the travelling mechanic case, for example, the parties might agree that the employee will be reinstated to his job subject to the contingency that if he has another accident due to his negligence while driving a company vehicle, he will be discharged.

Trade-offs

Many agreements are based upon trades in which each party gives up an interest of less importance to it in order to obtain an interest of more importance to it. This type of agreement is most likely when there are two or more interests involved, to which the parties attach different importance.

The More Issues, the Easier it Is to Reach Agreement

The inexperienced mediator who is faced with a dispute involving several issues may fear that with so many issues to be resolved, achieving overall agreement will be extremely difficult. In fact, multiple issues provide multiple opportunities for trade-offs, particularly when different interests are involved. Indeed, some mediators, faced with a single-issue dispute for which resolution is difficult, will seek to fractionate that issue — divide it into several issues — to create the opportunity for trade-offs. If, for example, there is a dispute limited to how much money A owes B, reaching agreement may be difficult because the parties have conflicting interests on that one issue — A wants to pay B as little as possible, B wants to receive as much as possible. If, however, A has complained that paying B is difficult because A's business is doing poorly, the mediator may ask A if he thinks business will improve. If so, the mediator may ask A if he could pay more if his payments were spread over time. If A says yes, and B has no immediate need for the money, an agreement should not be difficult. By dividing the single issue of how much A is to pay B into two issues — how much and when — an agreement based on a trade-off of time for money is achieved.

Agreements between Parties with a Continuing Relationship

If the parties have a continuing relationship, such as that between a landlord and a tenant association, a distributor and a retailer, or a union and an employer, they will have an interest in the effect of resolving one dispute on future disputes, as well as the effect of the settlement on their relationship. From one perspective, this complicates dispute resolution. But, as discussed above, additional issues create additional possibilities for trade-offs, making settlement less difficult. Some examples are the following:

Non-Precedent Setting Agreements. A party which is willing to enter into a settlement, but fears that the settlement can be used against it in future disputes between the same parties, can be protected against that risk by a clause guaranteeing that the agreement will not set a precedent in the event similar disputes arise in the future.

Narrow the Scope of the Issue in Dispute. Another means of assuring a party who is concerned about the future ramifications of a settlement is to narrow the scope of the issue dealt with in that settlement. For example, some claims are resolved by a settlement that grants the claim "under the circumstances of this case," but then sets out the circumstances in such a way that a similar situation would be unlikely to arise again.

Expand the Scope of the Issue in Dispute. Although narrowing the scope of the issue may lead to settlement, expanding the scope of the issue may not only result in a settlement, it may also resolve the problem underlying the dispute. In the travelling mechanic case, for example if there had been previous disputes growing out of determinations by the company's safety committee that the driver of a company vehicle had been negligent, the union representing the employees might agree to a particular settlement for the employee on the condition that one or more employee representatives be added to the company safety committee.

MEDIATOR PROPOSALS

If the parties are unwilling or unable to make acceptable proposals, the mediator may, but doing so is controversial. Some mediators believe that they should not make settlement proposals for fear of compromising their neutrality if the proposal is viewed as favoring one party over the other. Other mediators believe that a well-crafted mediator proposal coming at the right moment can be so valuable in reaching settlement that a ban on making such proposals is unwarranted. Some mediation programs may have policies on this issue. Absent any such policy, the key question is whether and when a mediator proposal should be made in a particular case.

There is general agreement that the mediator should refrain from making proposals until the parties have done so and none of their proposals have been mutually acceptable. If a mediator proposal comes before that, it may be viewed as indicating that the mediator is more interested in her own views of a sound settlement than in the views of the parties, and/or that the mediator has predetermined the "best" outcome. The mediator who delays making a settlement proposal until the parties have tried and failed to come up with a mutually acceptable agreement not only avoids this negative view of her proposal, but also benefits from the parties' greater willingness at that point to accept the view of a third party.

Mediator Proposals Designed to Overcome Reactive Devaluation

There is always a risk that parties will view any proposal coming from the other party with suspicion, fearing that it may contain hidden dangers: *Anything they propose can't be good for us.* The mediator may help overcome this mindset, known as reactive devaluation, by turning a party's proposal made during a separate session into a mediator proposal. Coming from the mediator, rather than a self-interested party, the proposal is more likely to be considered on its merits.

If the mediator is uncomfortable presenting one party's proposal as her own, she can say nothing about the origin of the proposal, asking only that it be considered on its merits. For example:

> Party (to Mediator): *Whose idea is this anyway?*

> Mediator: *Never mind that. Let's talk about it and see if it makes sense to you.*

Splitting the Difference

Some mediators will propose resolving a dispute by splitting the difference between the parties' positions. For example, such a mediator might say:

> *Mr. X, you think that that Ms. Y's actions caused damages to your business in the amount of $100,000, which is your settlement demand. Ms. Y, you think that Mr. X's business suffered at most $10,000 in damages, and that's the amount of your settlement offer. Why don't you resolve this matter by Ms. Y paying Mr. X $55,000, which is halfway between your two positions?*

If such a suggestion is made early in a mediation, it may be treated with disdain. *We didn't need to pay a mediator to tell us to split the difference. We could have done that ourselves if we thought it made sense.* If, however, the mediation has been going on for hours, and the parties have narrowed the gap between their initial positions from $90,000 (the difference between Mr. X's initial demand of $100,000 and Ms. Y's initial offer of $10,000), to a gap of $8,000 (with Mr. X demanding $53,000 and Ms. Y offering $45,000), they may both accept the mediator's suggestion that they split the difference and settle at $49,000. Each party will feel that it has been successful in persuading the other to make substantial concessions, both are likely to be fatigued, and splitting the small difference between them will appear a far sounder suggestion at this point than did splitting a larger difference early in the mediation.

ENCOURAGING EACH PARTY TO MAKE THE BEST OFFER IT CAN, CONSISTENT WITH ITS INTERESTS AND PRIORITIES

Sometimes a mediator may realize that a party's settlement proposal could be made more acceptable to the other party at no cost to the proposing party. This may occur when a party does not understand how its proposal might be improved without harming its own interests. It may also occur when, because of emotions stirred by the dispute, a party does not want to "reward" its opponent.

The case of the traveling mechanic provides some guidance on what a mediator might do in such a situation. The employer's response to the mediator's initial inquiry about the possibility of rehiring the discharged employee was *Not in a million years*. When the mediator asked about the employer's own statement that the employee was a good mechanic, the employer realized that offering reinstatement as a nondriving mechanic would both protect the company's safety interests and further its human resource interests by retaining an experienced and capable mechanic. Ultimately, the dispute was settled on that basis.

A party may be reluctant to make its best offer out of concern that the other party will see that offer as a sign of weakness, and will demand even more to settle. The mediator may overcome this barrier by offering to find out whether, if such an offer is made, it will be accepted. She can also reassure the reluctant party that she will do so without revealing that it is prepared to make such an offer:

Mediator (in caucus with Party A): *Would you be willing to pay $2 million to settle this matter?*

Party A: *Maybe, but I'm worried that if I offer $2 million, they'll just ask me for more. . . let me think about it.*

Mediator: *While you're thinking about it, let me see if they will settle at $2 million. . . But don't worry, I won't tell them you'll pay that much.*

Mediator (in caucus with Party B): *Sorry I was with Party A so long, but I'm really trying to get them to make an offer that you might accept. Let me ask you this. . . if they would go to $2 million, would that be enough to settle the matter?*

Party B: *Yes, we would, but have they told you they will go that high?*

Mediator: *Not yet, but I'm hopeful.*

Mediator (in caucus with Party A): *$2 million will do it. Can I communicate that offer?*

By protecting party A against the risk that party B would use its willingness to pay $2 million as a basis for demanding more, the mediator encouraged A to offer $2 million. The result is an agreement that is satisfactory to both parties.

AIDING EACH PARTY IN COMPARING THE BEST AGREEMENT AVAILABLE IN MEDIATION WITH THE BEST OUTCOME IT CAN REASONABLY EXPECT OUTSIDE MEDIATION (BATNA)

Parties sometimes have difficulty deciding whether to accept the other party's best offer or to pursue their BATNA. The mediator can help in two ways. First, she can encourage the uncertain party to evaluate the other party's offer (the best agreement available in mediation) in light of (1) its interests and priorities, (2) the agreement's likelihood of being successfully implemented, and (3) its likely durability. Second, the mediator can encourage the uncertain party to compare the best agreement available in mediation with the best outcome that party can reasonably expect outside mediation.

It is not uncommon for a party involved in a dispute to have an unrealistic view of its alternative to agreement in mediation. If the alternative is court, each party may have an overly optimistic view of its prospects of prevailing in the litigation. If the alternative is a power struggle — a strike or a commercial boycott — each may be convinced that it is the more powerful. The mediator may be able to help such parties see the risks and costs of their alternative to agreement in mediation. The mediator may also help the parties understand that they have control over the outcome in mediation, but that if they exit mediation without an agreement they will no longer have control over what happens. With a more realistic view of the situation in the event of no agreement, each party may be able to make a more reasoned decision concerning whether the best agreement it can attain in mediation is superior to its BATNA, particularly in view of the uncertainty of its attaining the latter.

There are two different means by which the mediator may encourage a more realistic view of the no-agreement situation. Some mediators do this by asking questions which are designed to encourage each party to focus on the realistic likelihood of attaining its BATNA, rather than an outcome far less desirable (sometimes referred to as the WATNA – Worst Alternative to a Negotiated Agreement). For example, the mediator might ask the employee in the travelling mechanic case how likely he thinks it is that a judge (or arbitrator) will order the company to reinstate him to a driving job in view of his past driving record. Other mediators prefer a more direct approach, which, in the travelling mechanic case, would have the mediator tell the employee that it is unlikely, in view of his driving record, that a judge or arbitrator would order his reinstatement to a driving job. (In the event that the employee is not represented in the mediation, ethical issues would be presented by the mediator giving the employee advice concerning the likely outcome in court or arbitration. See Mixed Professional Practices, page 89, for a discussion of those issues.) Still other mediators will begin with an indirect reality-testing approach, and, if that fails to alter the party's view, switch to a more direct approach.

The advantage of the direct approach is that it makes plain to the parties the mediator's view on the merits of the dispute, and so may have more effect than simply asking questions. The disadvantage of this approach is that once the mediator has said that one party is more likely than the other to be found "right," the mediator may be regarded by the other party as either incompetent or biased against it, either of which would diminish the mediator's credibility. Additionally, a party may be more convinced of the weakness of its position if it reaches that conclusion itself, as a result of the mediator's reality-testing questions, than if the mediator explicitly tells that party that she views his position as weak, a direct confrontation that may stir a defensive reaction.

Whichever approach the mediator favors, and this may differ depending on the context in which the mediation takes place, the mediator should remember that the ultimate responsibility for deciding whether to accept the best agreement available in mediation or to seek a better outcome outside mediation rests with the parties, whose dispute it is, not with the mediator. Indeed, the Model Standards of Conduct for Mediators (2005) provide in relevant part:

STANDARD 1. SELF-DETERMINATION

A. A mediator shall conduct a mediation based on the principle of party self-determination. Self-determination is the act of coming to a voluntary, uncoerced decision in which each party makes free and informed choices as to process and outcome....

B. A mediator shall not undermine party self-determination by any party for reasons such as higher settlement rates, egos, increased fees, or outside pressures.

Those mediators who assign the greatest weight to party self-determination are reluctant to offer any advice to parties on the ultimate question of whether they should accept the best offer available in mediation or their BATNA. Other mediators will offer advice on this question, but make no effort to persuade a party regarding its choice between the best agreement available in mediation and its BATNA. Still others view it as the mediator's function to bring the parties to agreement and will seek to persuade them to accept the best agreement available in mediation. For those mediators, persuasion constitutes neither coercion nor the undermining of party self-determination as those terms are used in the Model Standards.

Some parties may not wait until the latter stages of mediation to seek the mediator's agreement with their opinion that they are likely to prevail in court. The mediator should normally delay discussing this issue until there has been a thorough exploration of the parties' interests, and a substantial effort to develop a settlement. There are two reasons for delaying discussion of the strength of parties' alternative to agreement. First, the parties may be more creative if they are thinking about mutually acceptable settlements than if they are making arguments intended to persuade the mediator as to which of them is more likely to prevail in court or a power contest. Second, the mediator who reveals that she views one party as more likely to prevail in court or in a power struggle risks losing the confidence of the other party. For both these reasons, it is advisable to delay discussing the strength of disputants' BATNAs until efforts to resolve the dispute on the basis of their interests and priorities has been unsuccessful.

Ending the Mediation

Consistent with the voluntary nature of mediation, typically either party can end the mediation at any time. The exception is when the mediation takes place pursuant to a contractual agreement or court order which contains provisions other than allowing either party to terminate the mediation whenever it wishes to do so. The mediator will normally end the mediation if she believes the parties to be at an impasse, and that further discussion, at least until the parties have had an opportunity for reflection, is unlikely to be fruitful. Even then, the mediator may encourage the parties to continue negotiating on their own, and offer to participate in such negotiations if the parties wish her to do so.

Conclusion

Even when a mediator carefully follows all the systematic steps in the mediation process, from introducing the parties to the process and each other, explaining her role and the rules of mediation, difficulties may arise. For example, each party may be unwilling to make the first offer, blocking any movement; strong emotions may interfere with calm assessment of the alternatives to agreement; each party may be more interested in proving that it is right and the other wrong than in reaching agreement; or there may not be zone of possible agreement. Chapter 4 addresses these and other particularly difficult situations a mediator may face in seeking to assist disputing parties to find a mutually acceptable resolution of their dispute.

References

Friedman, G., & Himmelstein, J. (2008). *Challenging conflict: Mediation through understanding*. Chicago, IL: American Bar Association.

Goldberg, S. B., & Shaw, M. L. (2007). The secrets of successful (and unsuccessful) mediators continued: Studies two and three. *Negotiation Journal*, 23, 393–418.

Goldberg, S. B., Shaw, M. L., & Brett, J. M. (2009). What difference does a robe make? Comparing mediators with and without prior judicial experience. *Negotiation Journal, 25*, 277–305.

Model standards of conduct for mediators. (2005). http://www.americanbar. org/content/dam/aba/migrated/dispute/documents/model_standards_conduct_ april2007.authcheckdam.pdf

Swaab, R. I., & Brett, J. M. *Third parties resolving disputes: Building relationships and using substantive tactics in caucuses prior to joint meetings.* Working Paper.

Recommended DVDs Demonstrating Different Approaches to Mediation

CPR International Institute for Conflict Prevention & Resolution (1994, 2005). *Mediation in action: Resolving a complex business dispute* [DVD]. Available from CPR International Institute for Conflict Prevention & Resolution https:// www.cpradr.org/ or Dispute Resolution Research Center, Northwestern University http://www.kellogg.northwestern.edu/research/drrc/teaching-materials/ mediation-in-action.aspx. (A mediation that is primarily facilitative but also contains an evaluative component, conducted almost entirely in separate sessions).

Friedman, G. J., Himmelstein, J., & Mnookin, R. H. (2007). *Saving the last dance: Mediation through understanding* [DVD]. Available from Program on Negotiation at Harvard Law School http://www.pon.harvard.edu/shop/category/ audio-cd/. (An entirely facilitative mediation conducted by a mediator who does not use separate sessions.)

There are additional video resources cited at the end of Chapter 4.

Suggested Reading

American Arbitration Association. (2010). *AAA handbook on mediation* (2nd ed.). Huntington, NY: Juris Publishing.

Beer, J., & Packard, C. (Eds.). (2012). *The mediator's handbook* (4th ed.). Gabriola Island: New Society.

Boulle, L. (2011). *Mediation principles, process, practice* (3rd ed.). Chatswood: Butterworths.

Boulle, L., Colatrella, M., & Picccione, A. (2008). *Mediation skills and techniques.* Durham, NC: Carolina Academic Press.

Brown, G. (Ed.). (2016). Mediation practice: Challenges and new horizons. *Dispute Resolution Magazine, 3*, 22.

Fisher, R., Ury, W., & Patton, B. (2011). *Getting to yes: Negotiating agreement without giving in* (Rev. Ed.). New York, NY: Penguin Books

Golann, D. (2009). *Mediating legal disputes: Effective strategies for neutrals and advocates.* Chicago, IL: American Bar Association.

Hoffman, D. (2013). *A practice guide for mediators, lawyers, and other professionals*. Boston, MA: MCLE, Inc.

Kovach, K. K. (2008). *Mediation principles and practice* (3rd ed.). St. Paul, MN: West.

Moffitt, M., & Bordone, R. (Eds.). (2005). *The handbook of dispute resolution*. San Francisco, CA: Jossey-Bass.

Moore, C. W. (2014). *The mediation process: Practical strategies for resolving conflict* (4th ed.). San Francisco, CA: Jossey-Bass.

Pearson, J., & Thoennes, N. (1988). Divorce mediation research results. In J. Folberg & A. L. Milne (Eds.), *Divorce mediation: Theory and practice*. New York, NY: Guilford Press.

Stulberg, J. B., & Love, L. P. (2013). *The middle voice: Mediating conflict successfully* (2nd ed.). Durham, NC: Carolina Academic Press.

Mediation Provider Organizations

Though a number of organizations provide rules, suggested mediation clauses, and rosters of mediators at the regional level or for particular types of disputes (family, environmental, for example), the following organizations are national or international in scope and cover a wide variety of disputes. Their websites are rich sources of possible mediation clauses and freestanding agreements to mediate:

American Arbitration Association (AAA): http://www.adr.org

ADR Institute of Canada, Toronto: http:www.adric.ca

Beijing Arbitration Commission (BAC): http://www.bjac.org.cn/english/

Centre for Effective Dispute Resolution (CEDR): http://www.cedr.com/

Federal Arbitration, Inc., Palo Alto, CA: http://www.fedarb.com

Hong Kong International Arbitration Centre: http://www.hkiac.org

International Centre for Dispute Resolution, New York (associated with AAA): https://www.icdr.org

International Chamber of Commerce (ICC), Paris: http://www.iccwbo.org

International Institute for Conflict Resolution and Prevention (CPR), New York: http://www.cpradr.org

JAMS, Irvine, CA: http://www.jamsadr.com

London Court of International Arbitration (LCIA): http://www.lcia.org

Shanghai International Aviation Court of Arbitration (SHIAC): http://www.shiac.org/Aviation/aviation_news_detail_E.aspx?id=129

Singapore International Arbitration Centre (SIAC): http://www.siac.org.sg/

4 Dealing with Difficulties

There are some significant difficulties that mediators may encounter that are worthy of separate treatment. Among these are the following:

The Inability of the Disputing Parties to Reach Agreement

A difficulty that is of great concern to many mediators is the inability of the disputing parties to reach agreement. The following conversation between mediators would not be unusual:

> Mediator 1: *I had a really bad day today. I tried everything I know, but I still couldn't get an agreement. What worries me is that my low settlement rate may discourage people from hiring me.*

> Mediator 2: *I did OK today, but it's been a really tough week. I settled only one of my three mediations ... and I can't get the failures out of my mind. Maybe being a mediator is not for me.*

The assumption underlying the mediators' conversation is that agreement is the goal of both the mediation process and the mediator, and if no agreement has been reached both have failed.

A more nuanced, and we think more accurate, view is that disputing parties do go to mediation with the goal of reaching agreement — but only if they can obtain an agreement that each views as superior to its BATNA. For, it seems evident, a well-advised party will not accept an agreement in mediation if it views that agreement as inferior to its BATNA. It follows that the mediator's goal is not to assist the parties in reaching agreement, but rather to assist them in finding the best agreement possible in mediation, leaving it to each of them to decide if that agreement is better than its BATNA.

The mediator can assist each party in finding the best agreement possible in mediation by helping each to (1) understand its interests and priorities, as well as those of the other party, and (2) develop the best settlement proposal it is willing to make. Once each party has made its best settlement proposal, each knows the best agreement it can reach in mediation. At that point, it is for each party to compare the best agreement available in mediation with its BATNA and decide which it should choose. The mediator may aid the parties in making that comparison, and may, as discussed in Chapter 3, offer advice. But, even if the mediator thinks the best agreement available in mediation is superior to the parties' BATNA, his success as a mediator does not depend on whether or not the parties accept that agreement.

The mediator's role in this respect is not unlike that of a doctor treating an ill patient. The doctor's task is to provide a sound diagnosis of the illness and to recommend a course of treatment. If the patient decides not to follow that treatment, despite being advised of the risks of his decision, the doctor has not failed; the patient has exercised his right of free choice. So it is with mediation. If the mediator has done what he should to assist the parties in determining the best agreement possible in mediation, but one party prefers its BATNA, the mediator has not failed; the parties have exercised their right of free choice.

Acceptance of this more nuanced view of the mediator's role should have little effect on what the mediator actually does. The mediator techniques discussed in Chapter 3 and subsequently in this chapter are equally appropriate for the mediator who seeks to assist the parties in determining if they can reach an agreement that is better than their BATNA as they are for the mediator who believes it is his role to bring about agreement. As previously pointed out, those techniques consist of (1) aiding the parties in understanding their interests and priorities, as well as those of the other party; (2) using those interests and priorities to assist the parties in developing potential settlements; (3) encouraging the parties to make the best settlement offers possible; and (4) aiding each party in comparing the best agreement available in mediation with the best outcome it can reasonably expect outside mediation (BATNA).

Even though this alternative view of the mediator's goal may not affect the techniques he uses in a mediation, it should have a profound effect on how the mediator evaluates his success. The mediator who views his work as successful if he utilizes each of the techniques described above, without regard to whether the parties reach agreement, is free of self-imposed pressure to reach agreement. As a result, as Judge Brazil (2007) has pointed out, such a mediator is not subject to the temptation to manipulate the parties in order to obtain an agreement. He should not, for example, be tempted to exaggerate the weakness of each party's legal arguments, hoping thereby to make the potential agreement in mediation appear superior to court resolution. Nor should he be tempted to overstate the advantages of the best agreement available in mediation so as to encourage acceptance of that agreement.

Some mediators may be concerned that this approach will have a negative impact on their settlement rate, making them less attractive to parties selecting a mediator. That concern is unwarranted. Settlements obtained through mediator manipulation of the parties, even if they increase the mediator's settlement rate, are unlikely to increase his attractiveness as a mediator. The parties to a mediation and/or their lawyers or other representatives often engage in post-mediation discussion of the mediation and the mediator. If they discover that the mediator has engaged in the manipulative practice of telling each party that its case was a likely loser if the dispute were to go to trial, or that the mediator misstated his view of the advantages of settlement, they will not hesitate to criticize the mediator's behavior to others who ask whether they should use that mediator (Model Standards of Conduct for Mediators, 2005).

In sum, our view that the goal of the mediation process and the mediator is to assist each party in determining the best agreement available in mediation and whether that agreement is superior to its BATNA should have no effect on what the mediator does or how the mediator is viewed in the marketplace. It should, however, free the mediator from unwarranted pressure to obtain settlements and enable him to deal with the difficult moments in mediation free from such pressure.

One additional point... In Chapter 3, we wrote about techniques that the mediator may use to "help the parties reach settlement" or to "move the mediation towards settlement." We used these terms because it is simpler to say that the mediator is seeking settlement than that the mediator is seeking to assist each party in determining if the best agreement available in mediation is better than its BATNA. It should be clear, however, that whenever we suggest or encourage mediator behavior "designed to assist the parties in reaching settlement," we refer solely to behavior that assists the parties in determining if they can reach a settlement that each regards as superior to its BATNA.

We turn next to techniques that the mediator may use – in addition to those discussed in Chapter 3 – in dealing with difficulties encountered in mediation.

Unwillingness to Make the First Offer

At times, neither party is willing to make the first settlement offer. This often occurs when neither has a good sense of negotiation strategy and each fears being taken advantage of by the other. The mediator might address this situation by giving both parties advice on negotiation strategy. For example, the mediator might say to each (in separate sessions):

> One excellent way to determine your first offer is to identify the offer that is at the limit of what you can reasonably hope to attain. Such a first offer provides you with room to retreat and still end up with an acceptable agreement.... You must be prepared, however, for the other party to say, "How did you ever come up with that crazy proposal?" If you don't have a good answer to that question, your offer will not serve its intended purpose of starting the settlement negotiations where you would like them to start.

The mediator might also say:

> Another means of determining your first offer is to make it close to what you think would be a fair outcome, but with room to concede a bit and still end up with an acceptable outcome. If you start this way, you still must be prepared to provide a defensible answer to the

question, "How did you ever come up with that crazy proposal?" Developing that answer should not be difficult, however, because the proposal is not extreme.

By providing each party with a means for determining its first offer, the mediator should be able to break the deadlock of neither party being willing to make the first offer. Additionally, by giving each party the same tactical advice on making its first offer, the mediator eliminates any concern that he has prejudiced the outcome of the mediation by providing advice to only one party.

The mediator's suggestion that opening offers should leave room for subsequent concessions also signals to the parties that the mediation process will involve a series of offers and counter-offers, rather than "take it or leave it" proposals. This sets the stage for an orderly and productive interchange.

Strong Emotions

Parties who end up in mediation because they have been unable to resolve a dispute on their own are often angry and resentful. Such emotions are an obstacle to reasoned analysis, and being able to reason — to understand and weigh interests and priorities — is important to successful dispute resolution. Accordingly, the mediator needs to know how to manage emotions.

Efforts by the mediator to ignore parties' emotions or to persuade parties to suppress their emotions are unlikely to be successful. The key to turning an emotional party into one who is able to participate in reasoned settlement discussions is to let him express his emotions, signaling respect for his remarks by thoughtful questioning and empathic listening. Once the emotional party believes his concerns have been heard and respected, he is more likely to turn to the hard work of settlement negotiations. This means that the first step in successfully managing emotions consists of providing the parties with an opportunity to express ("vent") their emotions.

The mediator needs to decide whether venting should take place in joint session with the mediator and the other party or in a separate session alone with the mediator. There are pros and cons to each approach, and the mediator must decide on a case-by-case basis whether having the parties express their emotions directly to each other will help or hurt the mediation.

The advantage of venting in joint session is that speaking about one's anger, hurt, or disappointment directly to the other party in the presence of the mediator should help reduce the speaker's emotions. The risk is that the other party may become defensive and emotional in return, jeopardizing the mediation. One way to avoid this risk is for the mediator to discuss with the parties in private session whether a joint venting session is likely to be helpful:

> Mediator (to Party A): *I sense that you are very angry with [the other party] for her actions in this matter. Is that right?*

> Party A: *It certainly is. I can't believe that someone I trusted could do such a thing.*

> Mediator: *Sometimes it helps if the mediator provides each party with an opportunity to express her feelings to the other party and hear what she has to say in return. Would you like the opportunity to do that in this case?*

> Party A: *I certainly would.*

> Mediator: *And could you sit still and listen quietly while [the other party] responds, perhaps expressing her anger at you?*

> Party A: *Sure. I know what she's going say and it doesn't bother me at all.*

If both parties are interested in a joint venting session, and if each believably asserts that she can maintain her composure during such a session, the mediator may decide to schedule it. He can always cut the session short if it threatens to get out of control. The mediator may even use a failed venting session as a reason why resolving the dispute as soon as possible and so avoiding future interaction is in the self-interest of each.

If venting has not succeeded in calming the parties' emotions so that they can proceed with settlement negotiations, the mediator might suggest adjourning the mediation and asking each party to bring a "coach" to the next mediation session. The coach should be someone who can counsel the party whose emotions would otherwise preclude the rational consideration of outcomes.

Each Party Thinks Only of Proving It Is "Right" and the Other Party Is "Wrong"

If the mediation is evaluative, each party is expected to present evidence and argument to show that it is right and the other party is wrong. Such presentations allow the mediator to evaluate the strength of the parties' arguments, and to provide them with a neutral view of which is more likely to prevail if the matter goes to court.

If, however, the mediation is interest-based, there is little gained from parties making arguments to show they are right – at least not until interest-based efforts to reach agreement have proven unsuccessful. Nonetheless, such arguments are common in interest-based mediation, particularly at the outset. At times, this is because the parties do not fully understand the difference between focusing on rights and focusing on interests; at other times, it is because the parties or their lawyers are so accustomed to presenting their positions as a matter of "right" that they have difficulty doing otherwise. Whatever the reason, the presentation of rights-based arguments (whether orally or in written pre-mediation briefs) in the early stages of an interest-based mediation may distract the parties from focusing on their respective interests and priorities.

Some parties and their lawyers persist in making rights-based arguments throughout an interest-based mediation because they hope that the mediator will view their arguments as sound, and will rely on them to encourage the other party to modify its settlement position. At very least, they want the mediator to know that they are confident of their rights position and ready to go to court if their demands are not met – an outward show of strength.

The mediator who wishes to discourage this reliance on rights-based arguments might, in a separate session with a lawyer who insists his client has the stronger case, say something like:

> *The problem is that is exactly what [the other side] thinks. So if we're going to make any progress in this matter, I'm going to have to ask both parties to put aside the question of right and wrong – at least for now – and see if we can work out some kind of settlement that you could live with, that they could live with, and that probably would not involve them paying you [the amount you have demanded]. Let's just try, OK?*

Note that the mediator, by suggesting that the question of right and wrong should be put aside "for now" did not reject the lawyer's argument that he was right or foreclose him from raising that argument subsequently. The mediator also assured the lawyer that he was going to ask the other party to put aside rights-based arguments "for now." The combination of leaving the right/wrong question open for the lawyers to argue at a later time if an interest-based settlement cannot be reached, and treating each party alike should be enough to allow the mediator to refocus the discussion on the parties' interests rather than their rights.

The Parties Are Not Candid with the Mediator in Separate Session

Even when the mediator has emphasized the importance of the parties being candid with him when they are in separate session, they are sometimes reluctant to do so. They may not understand the importance of candor with the mediator or they may distrust his assurances of confidentiality.

If the parties' lawyers have previously worked with the mediator, he may ask them to encourage their clients to be candid with him, and to reassure them that they can do so without jeopardizing their case (though see Chapter 5 for some fine points on this). Still, there are times when the mediator must take the lead in encouraging parties to be candid. A mediator might say something like this to encourage full disclosure:

> I recognize that you may be reluctant to share information with me that you have not shared with the other party. You may fear that information will get back to them and weaken your bargaining position. But, if you tell me only what you tell the other party, you are not taking full advantage of what I can do to help you reach a settlement. If you will be candid with me about your needs and concerns, and what you really need for a satisfactory settlement, I can work with you to try to get a settlement that satisfies your most important needs, and that the other party can live with.
>
> I have promised that I will not tell the other side anything that you share with me in separate session without

your permission. Still, you may be wondering how you can trust me to keep that promise since you don't know me personally and we haven't worked together before this. The answer is quite simple. The mediation world is a small one ... If I breach my promise of confidentiality to you, you will tell others what I have done, and I may never work as a mediator again. As a result, it is in my personal interest to live up to my commitment to protect your confidence, and I will do so.

Behavioral Issues

Some disputants, particularly those who have no prior experience with mediation, may engage in behavior that, if left unchecked, could derail the mediation. This risk is particularly great if the disputants do not have a lawyer or other representative at the mediation.

THE PARTY WHO IS SILENT OR NEARLY SO

The mediator should address the reasons for the party's silence, taking her aside and asking:

I sense that you are having difficulty talking in this mediation. Can you tell me why?

If the direct approach is not successful, an indirect approach might work. The mediator might do some guessing:

I'm wondering if you are reluctant to talk because your supervisor is in the room.

I'm wondering if you are reluctant to talk because you are afraid you might say something that will hurt your case?

Getting a "yes" or "no" answer to such questions might allow the mediator to learn more with a follow-up "why?" question, or to craft assurances that make the silent party more comfortable in speaking. Alternatively, the answer to such questions might lead the mediator to continue the mediation in separate sessions.

THE PARTY WHO RAISES IRRELEVANT ISSUES

The mediator should not ignore a party's discussion of issues that appear irrelevant to the dispute. Instead, the mediator should follow up with questions aimed at determining if the party thinks the issue is relevant to the dispute. If not, the mediator should not pursue it. If so, the mediator may be able to use the interest disclosed by the party raising that issue as a trade-off in developing an interest-based proposal.

> Mediator: *You have frequently referred to your being on vacation at the time the bill became due. Does that have something to do with your not paying the bill?*
>
> Party: *No, I just thought it was curious that a bill for something I bought during last summer's vacation should arrive during this summer's vacation.*
>
> * * * * * * * * * * * * * *
>
> Mediator: *You mentioned that you had never before seen the form that your supervisor at the hospital asked you to fill out. Does that have something to do with your refusal to fill out the form?*
>
> Party: *Sure. I wasn't going to fill out a form that could result in losing my license.*
>
> Mediator: *I don't understand. Please explain it to me.*
>
> Party: *Sure. I'm a licensed EMT (Emergency Medical Technician) and the form asks for information that I think an EMT is not supposed to disclose to anyone without the patient's consent.*
>
> Mediator: *If your supervisor could get clearance from the licensing authority for you to disclose that information to the hospital, would you be willing to do so?*
>
> Party: *Sure.*

ONE PARTY ENGAGES IN DISRUPTIVE BEHAVIOR

One party (or both) may engage in behavior that renders a reasoned exchange of views next to impossible. Among such behavior may be continually interrupting the other party or bullying the other party by threats of physical force or criminal prosecution. The mediator who is faced with such conduct could remind the parties that they agreed to treat each other with respect. If this does not lead to prompt termination of the offensive behavior, the mediator could put the parties in separate rooms. Doing so may permit the mediator to help a party reflect on his own self-interest in terminating the offensive behavior:

> *I wonder what you think [the other party's] reactions are to what you have just said. .... Perhaps a part of you wants to say that and see their reaction. Let me ask you a question, though. Do you want to get this matter resolved today? Because if you do, you're going to have to stop [the disruptive behavior]. Do you think you can do that? If you can, we'll continue the mediation; if not, I'll have to terminate it.*

If the mediator believes that the offensive behavior has fatally compromised the possibility of free and uncoerced decision-making, he can terminate the mediation without giving the offending party a choice.

The Mediator Who Finds One Party More Sympathetic or Appealing

Mediators, despite their obligation to act with complete neutrality, are only human, and may find one party more sympathetic or appealing than the other. Such a preference, of itself, is no cause for concern ... as long as the mediator is capable of maintaining his neutral appearance and behavior. If he cannot do so, he should withdraw as mediator, explaining to the parties the reason for his withdrawal (although not necessarily which party he finds more sympathetic or appealing).

The Mediation Appears to Be at Impasse

When a mediation appears to be at impasse, the mediator needs to consider (1) whether the seeming impasse reflects an informed decision by one or both parties that the best agreement that can be obtained by it in mediation is inferior to the best outcome reasonably available to it outside the mediation; (2) whether, in view of the parties' interests and priorities, there is no zone of potential agreement (ZOPA); or (3) whether, in the mediator's judgment, the dispute could be resolved in a fashion that would satisfy the core interests of both parties without either of them running the risk of resort to an uncertain BATNA. If the mediator's conclusion is the latter, there are a number of techniques open to the mediator to attempt to break the impasse, none of which involve the mediator bringing pressure on the parties to do anything other than make an informed decision whether or not to settle.

Zone of Potential Agreement: ZOPA

If the maximum that one party, such as the defendant in a lawsuit, is willing to pay to settle that suit is $50,000, and the minimum the plaintiff is willing to accept is $45,000, there is a zone of potential agreement (ZOPA) between $45,000 and $50,000. If the maximum that the defendant is willing to pay is $50,000, and the minimum that the plaintiff is willing to accept is $55,000, there is no ZOPA.

Even when there is a ZOPA, parties sometimes fail to discover it because one or the other is unwilling to disclose the best offer it would make to obtain a settlement. For example, the defendant might be unwilling to disclose its willingness to pay $50,000. In order to overcome that barrier to a settlement that would serve the interests of both parties the mediator will encourage each to make the best offer it is willing to make to obtain an agreement.

BRINGING THE PARTIES TOGETHER FOR A FINAL TRY AT REACHING AGREEMENT

If the mediator has been meeting with the parties primarily in separate sessions, he should consider bringing them together for a final face-to-face meeting before terminating the mediation. In such a meeting, each party, faced with the prospect of no agreement, and having before it what it almost surely regards as an intransigent opponent, may loudly and aggressively point out the advantages of its most recent settlement offer and the dire consequences to the other party of not accepting that offer. The other party may respond in kind, with the result that one of the parties, with no pressure from the mediator, will rethink its view on either the advantages of settlement or the disadvantages of no agreement, leading to a settlement that each party views as preferable to its BATNA. Alternatively, one or both parties, faced with the prospect of the imminent termination of the mediation, may alter its last settlement proposal, also leading to a mutually acceptable agreement.

It is also possible that the frustration of each party at being confronted with its seemingly intransigent opponent may result in heightened emotions and an abrupt end to the mediation. Accordingly, the mediator should reserve this technique for the closing moments of a mediation that appears, absent some dramatic intervention, to be headed for an impasse.

WARNING THE PARTIES THAT THE MEDIATOR WILL TERMINATE THE MEDIATION IF NO AGREEMENT IS REACHED BY A CERTAIN DATE OR TIME

A mediator may try to restart a stalled mediation by telling the parties that unless they have reached agreement (or made significant progress toward agreement) by a certain date or time, he will terminate the mediation. The mediator who uses this approach hopes that it will lead to settlement. However, like bringing the parties together for a last-ditch face-to-face discussion, this approach does no more than put pressure on the parties to reach a decision on whether or not to settle, free from mediator pressure to do either.

A MEDIATOR SETTLEMENT PROPOSAL

As previously pointed out, many mediators are reluctant to make settlement proposals for fear that the terms of such a proposal may appear to one party to be more favorable to the other, causing the former to view the mediator as biased against it and so reducing the mediator's effectiveness. When the mediator is faced with an apparent impasse and the termination of the mediation, the mediator's potential loss of effectiveness if his settlement proposal is rejected is of little consequence. Under these circumstances, most mediators are willing to make a settlement proposal.

Some mediators base their settlement proposals on their view of a fair resolution of the dispute, taking into account the interests and priorities of each party, as well as their respective

BATNAs. Other mediators base their settlement proposals on their view of what the parties are likely to accept. Whichever of these approaches the mediator uses, each party is free to reject the mediator's proposal. As a result, the principle that the mediator's function is to assist the parties in making an informed decision whether or not to settle, rather than pressuring them to settle, is not violated by a mediator proposal.

In making an impasse-breaking proposal at the end of a mediation, the mediator may set the following ground rules: (1) The parties can either accept or reject the mediator's proposal, but there will be no further negotiations after the proposal has been made; (2) the parties will inform only the mediator, not each other, of their responses to his proposal; (3) the mediator will not announce the parties' decisions unless both parties accept the proposal. These ground rules, taken together, are intended to eliminate the parties' fear that a "yes" response by one party to the mediator's proposal will be taken by the other as a sign of weakness, encouraging the other party to say "no" in the hope of reopening negotiations and driving a harder bargain.

An alternative approach to encouraging agreement, with less mediator involvement in the terms of the agreement, is for the mediator to propose a range within which settlement negotiations will continue. This technique is most often used when (1) the sole or primary issue is the amount one party must pay the other to settle the dispute; (2) the parties began the mediation far apart on that issue; and (3) subsequent negotiations have not narrowed the gap sufficiently that agreement appears likely.

Assume for example, that a dispute over a defect in the construction of a building has led to a lawsuit by the building owner against the construction company. The building owner begins the mediation by demanding $2 million in damages; the construction company responds by offering $50,000 to settle what it characterizes as a "nuisance suit." In the course of 4 hours of mediation, the building owner reduces its demand from $2 million to $1.75 million, and then to $1.25 million; the construction company increases its offer from $50,000 to $100,000, and then to $350,000. After another 2 hours of mediation neither party has altered its last position and a negotiated agreement appears unlikely.

At this point, the mediator may ask the parties if they are willing to have him propose a settlement range within which further negotiations will take place. The mediator should explain that he will propose the range in a joint session, but their responses will be given only to the mediator. If each tells him privately that it is willing to continue negotiations within the proposed range, the mediation will continue. If one party is not willing to continue negotiations within that range, the mediator will announce that the mediation has ended, but not which party has rejected the proposed settlement range. Since authorizing the mediator to propose a range does not oblige a party to accept the mediator's proposed range, much less accept a particular figure within that range, parties who genuinely want to settle are often willing to allow the mediator to propose a settlement range.

In choosing the settlement range, the mediator is likely to be guided by his sense of the range in which a settlement, if any, is likely to occur. The mediator will also want to make the range sufficiently narrow that the parties' acceptance of it represents significant progress toward agreement. If, in the situation described above, the mediator proposed a range of $500,000–$1 million, the parties would still be so far apart that further negotiations would be unlikely to be fruitful. Conversely, a range such as $650,000–$850,000, if accepted, would put the parties sufficiently close that agreement becomes substantially more likely. (Because this approach does not involve the mediator proposing a specific agreement, but only a range, some mediators do not wait for an impasse to use it, but will do so earlier in the mediation to stimulate progress.)

If negotiations within the agreed-upon range do not produce agreement, the mediator may then ask the parties if they would like him to make a specific proposal for settlement. He should reiterate the ground rules regarding confidentiality of their responses and that no further negotiations will take place after their responses are received.

Some mediators provide the parties with reasons for their proposed settlement ranges or numbers; others do not. Those who provide reasons believe that doing so enhances the likelihood their proposals will be accepted; those who do not believe that giving reasons serves only to provide a justification for rejection by a party which does not want to settle.

The Parties Reach a Tentative Agreement that the Mediator Views as Unfair to One of Them

At times, parties are willing to accept a settlement that the mediator believes is unfair to one of them. One example would be a divorce mediation in which the wife is ready to agree to her husband's proposals for alimony and child support that the mediator believes to be far less than she would receive if the matter went before a judge. The mediator might:

- Suggest that the parties take time for reflection before finalizing the agreement, and in the meantime discuss the matter with a family member, a friend, or a lawyer. Even if this delay results in no mediated agreement, it may be better for both parties, even the husband (see below), than a grossly unfair agreement reached in mediation.
- Meet privately with the party that stands to benefit from the unfair agreement, suggesting that such an agreement may not be as advantageous as it seems because the other party might ultimately refuse to abide by what it views as an unfair agreement. Even if the party that stands to benefit may ultimately be able to force compliance, it might be better off with a less favorable agreement that the other party complies with willingly. The mediator might even suggest some modifications in the proposed agreement that would accomplish that goal.
- The mediator should not seek to dissuade the weaker party from signing the proposed agreement, as doing so would violate the mediator's duty of neutrality between the parties. This is not the case when the mediator merely asks the stronger party, in private, if it might not be in that party's own interest to amend the proposed agreement.

We turn next, in Chapter 5, to the relationship between the mediation process and the law.

References

Brazil, W. D. (2007). Hosting mediations as a representative of the system of civil justice. *Ohio State Journal on Dispute Resolution, 22,* 227–276.

Model standards of conduct for mediators. (2005). http://www.americanbar. org/content/dam/aba/migrated/dispute/documents/model_standards_conduct_ april2007.authcheckdam.pdf

Recommended Mediation Demonstration DVDs

American Bar Association Section on Dispute Resolution, & Suffolk University Law School Dispute Resolution Video Center (n.d.). *Dispute resolution video center.* Retrieved from http://www.adrvideo.org/. (The ABA Section on Dispute Resolution and Suffolk Law School have cooperated to create and maintain a website listing dispute resolution videos).

CPR International Institute for Conflict Prevention & Resolution. (1994, 2005). *Mediation in action: Resolving a complex business dispute* [DVD]. Available from CPR International Institute for Conflict Prevention & Resolution: https:// www.cpradr.org/ or Dispute Resolution Research Center, Northwestern University: http://www.kellogg.northwestern.edu/research/drrc/teaching-materi- als/mediation-in-action.aspx

Frenkel, D. N., & Stark, J. H. (2008). *The practice of mediation: A video-inte- grated text* [DVD & Text]. New York, NY: Aspen Publishers.

Friedman, G. J., Himmelstein, J., & Mnookin, R. H. (2007). *Saving the last dance: Mediation through understanding* [DVD]. Available from Program on Negotiation at Harvard Law School: http://www.pon.harvard.edu/shop/cate- gory/audio-cd/

Mediation Research and Education Research Project, Inc. (MREP). (1991). *Grievance mediation in action* [DVD]. Available from MREP: http://www.mrep. org/index.html

Suggested Reading

Denlow, M. (2000). Breaking impasses in settlement conferences: Five techni- ques for resolution. *Judges' Journal*, 5–10.

Denlow, M. (2011). Breaking impasses in judicial settlement conferences: Seven (more) techniques for resolution. *Court Review*, 46, 130–134.

5 Mediation and the Law

Nancy H. Rogers*

T his chapter discusses laws that affect the mediation process and the conduct of the mediation.[1] If you are serving
as a mediator, the mediation-related laws most likely to
concern you fit into the following groups:

1. Encouraging disputants to be candid in mediation
   (confidentiality)
2. Disputants' obligations to attend and engage in mediation
3. Mediators' obligations to act impartially and with clarity
   and integrity
4. Preservation of the disputants' free choice regarding whether
   to settle in mediation
5. Mediation quality enhancement
6. Protection for the justice system's role and reputation.

---

*Nancy H. Rogers is coauthor of an earlier volume, *Mediation: Law,
Policy & Practice* with Sarah R. Cole, Craig A. McEwen, James R.
Coben & Peter N. Thompson. This chapter draws on this earlier work
with the authors' and publisher's permission.
[1]"Law" as used here is a broad category that includes statutes, regulations issued by administrative agencies, court rules, ethics provisions
adopted by a jurisdiction, and court rulings (often called the "common
law"). Laws have in common that courts and other legal authorities will
enforce them. Thus, lawyers may distinguish legal requirements (or law)
from other admonitions that sound like law, such as community mediation program rules, by saying the former have the "force of law."

If you are a mediation party, you will probably be most concerned with laws regarding confidentiality ("encouraging disputants to be candid in mediation") and "disputants' obligations to attend and engage in mediation" (the first two titled subparts below), though your mediation may raise additional legal issues not covered by this chapter. For example, drafting settlement agreements (whether or not reached through mediation) might involve consideration of tax consequences, antitrust issues, requirements to put the agreements in writing, clarity of terms, and when court approval is needed.

Legislatures, courts, and administrative agencies support and regulate mediation in pursuit of a variety of goals and concerns. Understanding these goals and concerns will help you anticipate legal issues not included in this chapter.

Lawmakers' reasons for supporting mediation and their concerns regarding mediation-related law might include:

- Mediation can reduce the average time from the beginning of the dispute to settlement, but only if conducted early in the life of the dispute.
- Early mediation, in turn, helps control the public costs for adjudication. It also tends to reduce the disputants' costs, but only if mediation fees are appropriate to the amounts at stake and the disputants' financial abilities.
- Most disputants react positively to mediation, so high quality mediation has the potential to maintain and even to improve the public's view of the justice system. This will require that the public views mediation as accessible regardless of wealth, as not preventing the disputants from litigating if they do not settle, and as administered without favoritism.
- In employment discrimination and family disputes, mediation is more likely than negotiation without a mediator to restore relationships, produce settlements that fit the disputants' needs, and generate commitment to comply with the agreement. Mediation should be used in family cases only if there are special provisions for cases involving abuse. (Cole, McEwen, Rogers, Coben, & Thompson, 2014–2015, §§ 2:1-9; 14:1-13, 15:2)

In addition to understanding the policies underlying the laws governing mediation generally, both mediators and parties benefit by being familiar with the law that affects the particular type of mediation involved (e.g., employment discrimination). You will also want to be familiar with the statutes, regulations, court rules, and legal precedents regarding mediation in three jurisdictions: (1) the one in which the mediation will be conducted; (2) the one in which the mediated agreement will be enforced; and (3) with respect to confidentiality, the ones in which information from the mediation might be sought.

Source of Mediation and the Law Summaries

You can access summaries of the law relating to mediation in legal treatises (Cole et al., 2014–2015; Nolan-Haley, 2013); online legal research tools[2]; court or agency websites[3]; and other sources cited throughout and at the end of this chapter.

Encouraging Disputants to Be Candid in Mediation

Several of the mediator techniques discussed in this book are intended to encourage disputants to be candid, that is, open and honest, in mediation. Three types of law play a central role in supporting candor in mediation. The first is law providing for a *mediation privilege,* the second is law related to *confidentiality agreements,* and the third is law imposing *mediator responsibilities regarding confidentiality.*[4] Though supporting candor lies at

---

[2]See, for example, https://1.next.westlaw.com/Browse/Home/Secondary Sources/TextsTreatises/AlternativeDisputeResolutionTextsTreatises/ MediationLawPolicyPractice?originationContext=typeAhead&context Data=(sc.Default)&transitionType=CategoryPageItem

[3]See, for example, https://www.sconet.state.oh.us/JCS/disputeResolu tion/resources/default.asp. (You might search through Google or another search engine using the name of your state and "mediation law.")

[4]Additional laws may be raised in an attempt to block use of mediation communications at a hearing (e.g., Federal Rules of Evidence 408 concerning compromise discussions and 801-807 concerning out-of-court statements) or to avoid disclosure during discovery (e.g., Federal Rule of Civil Procedure 26(b) permitting the court to weigh the need for the information against the burden of providing it). However, the application of these laws depends on circumstances of the later litigation, so they provide little guidance to the mediator or mediation parties at the time that mediation occurs.

the heart of these laws, sometimes the desire to promote another policy, such as assuring the accuracy or fairness of criminal judgments or the transparency of public decision-making, prevails over the candor goal.

MEDIATION PRIVILEGE

A mediation privilege allows specified participants to block use of mediation discussions in subsequent legal proceedings, such as in discovery and at trial. Mediation privileges vary by jurisdiction and type of mediation. Some jurisdictions (e.g., some federal courts with respect to federal issues) do not recognize a mediation privilege at all. Other jurisdictions recognize a mediation privilege only for specific types of mediation, such as court-connected mediation or employment-related mediation (Cole et al., 2014–2015, §§ 8:18, 8:19).

Privileges typically protect only mediation communications, though "communications" can include written as well as verbal communications and even those gestures that are intended as communications. The disputants' attendance and other noncommunicative facts (such as whether one disputant stumbled and had slurred speech) commonly fall outside the privilege's protection (Cole et al., 2014–2015, § 8:24). Typically, the parties can "waive" (surrender) the privilege (sometimes only in writing and with the acquiescence of the mediator and other participants), thus allowing what was said in mediation to be used in legal proceedings.

Variations in privilege law from one jurisdiction to the next appear most often when the policy of encouraging candor in mediation clashes with another public policy, such as:

- Requiring certain professionals to report abuse, neglect, or exploitation of children or protected adults.
- Requiring attorneys to report ethics violations committed by other attorneys.
- Encouraging mediation participants to report mediator misconduct.
- Accommodating disputants if they want to raise traditional contract defenses against enforcement of the mediated settlement, particularly defenses based on fraud and duress. For example, the Uniform Mediation Act allows use of mediation communications when a party challenges a mediated contract

and the person seeking to use mediation communications demonstrates to the tribunal that no other evidence on this point exists and that the need to use that evidence "substantially outweighs the interest in protecting confidentiality" (Uniform Mediation Act, § 6(b), 2001). (The California privilege, in contrast, makes no exception for this situation (California Evidence Code § 1119).)

- Providing for transparency of public decision-making through public meetings and records laws.
- Promoting fair judgments, especially for felony cases where the consequences of wrongful convictions or acquittals are particularly serious. For example, a Florida court allowed a man charged with attempted murder to depose (ask questions during discovery) a mediator on whether the alleged victim had threatened the defendant's life during a mediation session. If the mediator confirmed this, the defendant wanted to use the mediator's testimony at trial to support his claim of self-defense (*State v. Castellano*, 460 So. 2d 480 (Fla. App. 1984)). California accommodates such situations by making the privilege inapplicable in criminal proceedings while the Uniform Mediation Act provides a weighing process for determining admissibility in proceedings concerning serious (felony) charges (California Evidence Code § 1119: Uniform Mediation Act, § 6(b), 2001).
- Avoiding situations where people use the secrecy of a mediation session to hide discussions about how to commit a crime.
- Making certain that threats of violence can be revealed, even if made during mediation.
- Establishing whether the disputants negotiate in good faith during mediation. (Only some legal authorities recognize this as an important policy.) (Cole et al., 2014–2015, §§ 9:4-9, 8:23-28, 8:42-45).

When policies clash, jurisdictions often reach different conclusions about whether to carve out an exception to the mediation privilege. In the event that a mediation will cover highly sensitive information, these policy clashes are indications that legal research might be necessary, not only in the law of the state where the mediation occurred but also in the law of the state or federal jurisdiction where someone may seek to use mediation communications.

Reach of the Uniform Mediation Act

The Uniform Mediation Act is *not* law within a particular state unless adopted as a statute by that state's legislature or as a rule of evidence by its highest court or legislature. At the time this book was written, the District of Columbia, Hawaii, Idaho, Illinois, Iowa, Nebraska, New Jersey, Ohio, South Dakota, Utah, Vermont, and Washington had enacted the Uniform Mediation Act; in other words, it carries the force of law only in those 12 jurisdictions (additional enactments can be tracked at http://www.uniform-lawcommission.com/Act.aspx?title=Mediation%20Act).

At times, a mediation privilege may prevent disputants from using mediation communications in ways that appear entirely legitimate. For example, the mediation privilege may block a disputant's attempt to gain enforcement of an oral (unwritten and unrecorded) settlement agreement because the court may not permit anyone to testify about what was said during the mediation. As a result, disputants are often well-advised to write and sign (or the digital equivalent) their settlement agreement so that each may rely on the settlement being enforced (Cole et al., 2014–2015, §§ 7:5, 8:25).

Importantly, a mediation privilege typically prevents disclosure only in legal proceedings, not elsewhere. This means that if mediation participants want to speak during mediation without fear that what they say will appear in the media or other settings where the mediation privilege does not apply, they must enter into a confidentiality agreement.

CONFIDENTIALITY AGREEMENTS

A confidentiality agreement commonly prohibits those signing it from revealing mediation communications in any setting (not just the legal proceedings covered by a mediation privilege). Confidentiality agreements thus promote candor in ways that privilege laws alone typically do not. The disputants and the mediator may agree, for example, not to disclose mediation communications, not to subpoena such communications for use in legal proceedings, to let the other disputant know if someone seeks information from the mediation, and to require the mediator and all disputants to return certain confidential information provided for the mediation (for a more extensive list, see Scanlon, 1999, pp. 28–36).

The courts will generally enforce confidentiality agreements by awarding damages when one party to the agreement harms another by disclosing information that they agreed to keep confidential. In order to avoid lengthy squabbles about the amount of the harm caused by a violation of the confidentiality agreement, the parties can quantify in the agreement what a party must pay (known as "liquidated damages") if found in violation.

A couple of warnings are in order regarding confidentiality agreements. These agreements bind only those who sign them. Furthermore, signers cannot, by agreement, create a mediation privilege – even one that applies just to the signers – when the law does not provide for a privilege. This means that the courts will not consider themselves bound by the confidentiality agreement if a party to litigation subpoenas pertinent evidence of mediation communications or requests them through discovery (Cole et al., 2014–2015, §§ 8:37-39). As the courts see it, a confidentiality agreement that would keep pertinent evidence from a court is an agreement to suppress evidence and therefore in conflict with public policy. The courts commonly refuse to allow the confidentiality agreement to block use of evidence except in the rare case in which they decide that one party to the agreement tried to mislead the other party by agreeing not to subpoena evidence and then doing so (Cole et al., 2014–2015, §§ 8:37-39).

Because a confidentiality agreement extends beyond the protection provided by a mediation privilege, the mediator and disputants often enter a confidentiality agreement prior to mediation even if they believe that the mediation communications will be privileged. Later, people sometimes regret having signed an overly broad confidentiality agreement. Mediators may help avoid this problem by encouraging the parties to include exceptions in the confidentiality agreement that permit them to disclose what they would feel irresponsible keeping secret, for example, statements indicating child neglect or threats of physical harm.

MEDIATOR RESPONSIBILITIES REGARDING CONFIDENTIALITY
Lawmakers also encourage candor during mediation by requiring the mediator to maintain the confidentiality of mediation communications.

When mediation occurs during litigation, a court order or court rule might require the mediator (and also the parties) to avoid disclosing mediation communications (Cole et al., 2014–2015, § 8:47). Even outside of litigation, the Model Standards of Conduct for Mediators (Standard V, 2005) and most similar codes impose a duty on the mediator to maintain the disputants' expectations about confidentiality. The admonitions to maintain confidentiality apply when shuttling from one caucus to the other unless a disputant has given permission to share information from the caucus with another disputant. They are also important for mediators to remember when they write or speak about mediation and even when a judge asks informally how the mediation went. In addition, the Uniform Mediation Act prohibits mediator disclosures to a judge or other official who might make a decision on the dispute if no settlement is reached (Uniform Mediation Act, § 7, 2001).

Applicability of the Model Standards of Conduct for Mediators

Even in states in which the Model Standards (2005) have not been adopted as law, the Standards are gaining acceptance as gauges of reasonable conduct. The American Bar Association, Association for Conflict Resolution, and American Arbitration Association have endorsed the Standards. Courts therefore may one day use the Model Standards as a guide for liability when a mediator fails to abide by them and, as a result, causes harm to a disputant (Moffitt, 2003, p. 89). The Model Standards of Practice for Family and Divorce Mediation, approved by the ABA in 2001, provide well-accepted standards for that type of mediation practice.

The Model Standards also make the mediator responsible for promoting the disputants' understanding of their confidentiality obligations (Standard V.C., 2005). Mediators develop their own statements to comply with this obligation, depending on the law and circumstances, such as:

I will not voluntarily say anything about what is said during mediation – absent threats of violence, plans to commit a crime, and a few other narrow exceptions in the mediation privilege statute. Do you understand that through your confidentiality agreement you, too, have undertaken an obligation not to say anything outside this mediation about what was said here?

Because of the mediator's confidentiality obligations, mediators commonly make certain that they have the parties' written authorization to disclose mediation communications outside the mediation. For example, they might sign something like the following:

The undersigned agree that the mediator should tell the court that we will complete discovery by the end of this month and by next month will be ready for trial.

Disputants' Obligations to Attend and Engage in Mediation

Disputants are not required by law to settle their dispute in mediation, but the law may require them to attend mediation and sometimes to participate in discussions. Examples include:

- Courts and public agencies often have the authority to compel parties to mediate (Cole et al., 2014–2015, §§ 9:1-3).
- In some contexts, a statute requires or rewards the use of mediation before a disputant sues (Cole et al., 2014–2015, §§ 9:1-3).
- The courts also tend to enforce an agreement to mediate, even if one of the disputants did not notice the mediation clause, as not uncommonly occurs in a purchase agreement or an employment contract (Cole et al., 2014–2015, §§ 6:1-7). However, the courts generally will not enforce such form agreements if they rule them to be "unconscionable" – such as contained in a "take-it-or-leave-it" contract and either too expensive or weighted too heavily against one of the disputants (Cole et al., 2014–2015, § 6:7).
- Some statutes even require certain kinds of agreements (e.g., joint custody agreements in Arizona, disability provider contracts in Kansas) to include mediation clauses (Cole et al., 2014–2015, § 6:1; Kansas Statutes Annotated § 39-1806; Arizona Revised Statutes Annotated § 25-403.02).

Thus, many disputants arrive at mediation because they must.

Requirements to participate in mediation have the potential advantage of scheduling mediation early in the disputing process, when the disputants can still save time, money, and disruption by settling. In a number of studies, those required to mediate did not settle any less frequently than those attending mediation voluntarily, and both groups were equally positive about the experience (Cole et al., 2014–2015, § 14:3). At the same time, mandatory mediation can generate unnecessary expense when it is clear that disputants will not settle. In addition, some parties – notably victims of intimate partner violence – may view mediation as an avenue that the violent party will use to intimidate them. As a result, courts tend to excuse victims from mandatory mediation (Adkins, 2010, p. 101).

Those drafting mediation clauses for contracts commonly make mediation a "step" in a series of dispute resolution processes, as mentioned above (Chapter 2). You can find "form" versions of step clauses on the websites of mediation provider organizations (see Chapter 3, page 57).

Mediation clause drafters differ on the answers to a series of questions related to mandatory mediation. Variations in the law regarding mandatory mediation also occur frequently regarding these points:

- Should disputants who have lawyers be required to attend mediation with their lawyers (*see* Riskin, 1991; Wise, 2006, p. 858)?
- When should mediation occur with respect to: the filing of litigation (or arbitration or public agency proceedings), a stage of formal discovery, or another step in the process (Cole et al., 2014–2015, § 14:18)?
- Must the disputants' representatives come with settlement authority, and what does that mean (Sherman, 1993, pp. 2108–2111)?
- Should the disputants be required not only to attend mediation but also to negotiate in good faith during mediation? (see Thompson, 2011 (no); Brazil, 2000, pp. 31–33 (no); Lande, 2002 (no); Uniform Mediation Act, 2001 (no); Kovach, 1997, p. 583 (yes)). If so, what does that mean for confidentiality (the first titled subpart above), the parties' free choice concerning settlement (the section entitled, "Preservation of the Disputants' Free Choice Regarding

Whether to Settle in Mediation"), and mediator impartiality (the subpart immediately following this one)?

- Should the disputants' attorneys be required to submit written summaries of the facts and law involved in the case prior to mediation (Cole et al., 2014–2015, § 9:7)?
- How long should disputants be required to participate in mediation (Cole et al., 2014–2015, § 9:10)?
- Should disputants who are required to participate in mediation also have to pay for it (Brazil, 1999)?

Mediators' Obligations to Act Impartially and with Clarity and Integrity

A number of laws are designed to limit a mediator's ability to abuse the trust that she develops with the disputants. Among them are laws requiring mediators to disclose conflicts of interest; discouraging fee structures that could encourage mediators to steer settlements in particular ways; and prohibiting the mediator from exaggerating with respect to experience, training, and role.

CONFLICTS OF INTEREST

Conflicts of interest may affect a mediator's impartiality or the disputants' perception of impartiality. As a result, a variety of laws require mediators to disclose conflicts of interest to the disputants before mediation begins, and also if conflicts of interest surface during the course of mediation (e.g., Uniform Mediation Act § 9, 2001; Model Standards of Conduct for Mediators, Standard III, 2005). According to the Uniform Mediation Act (§ 9), the mediator shall:

> make an inquiry that is reasonable under the circumstances to determine whether there are any known facts that a reasonable individual would consider likely to affect the impartiality of the mediator, including a financial or personal interest in the outcome of the mediation and an existing or past relationship with a mediation disputant or foreseeable participant in the mediation....

Under the Model Standards of Conduct for Mediators, a mediator should not mediate a dispute if the conflict of interest is so severe that it undermines the integrity of mediation (Standard III, 2005). For example, a New Jersey court would not allow a "guardian ad litem"[5] for the children of divorced parents to mediate between the parents because a guardian is expected to make recommendations to the court and a mediator is required to maintain confidences (*Isaacson v. Isaacson*, 792 A.2d 525, 533–536 (App. Div. 2002)).

Mediators should avoid post-mediation relationships with any of the participants "that would raise questions about the integrity of the mediation," according to the Model Standards (Standard III, 2005). For example, a lawyer-mediator who has mediated a dispute between two parties should not represent either of them afterward on a legal matter related to the subject of the mediation. In addition, the lawyer-mediator's entire law firm will sometimes be precluded from representing either of the parties after the mediation. In other instances, the law firm can do so only if it erects barriers to prevent the mediator from sharing information with others in the firm and from receiving fees generated by the firm's representation (Cole et al., 2014–2015, § 10:5-7). For similar reasons, a mediator should not accept employment with either party right after the mediation.

FEE STRUCTURE

The mediator's fee structure might create a perception of conflict of interest or might impair impartiality. For example, a mediator's fee that is contingent on settlement might encourage the mediator to slant communications so that the disputants will settle. To avoid this, the Standards discourage contingent fees (Standard VIII.B., 2005). The Standards also encourage mediators to assess whether an unequal fee payment from the disputants, with one party paying more of the mediator's fee than the other, would make the mediator partial to the former (Cole et al., 2014–2015, § 10:5-7). However, this situation is not unusual if one disputant has more ability to pay, such as in mediations between large corporations and their employees.

---

[5]A neutral person appointed by the court to look into what the court should do to serve the children's interests and make a report to that effect to the court.

MIXED PROFESSIONAL PRACTICES

Mediators can often use professional skills in addition to their mediation skills without creating legal or ethical issues. For example, some lawyer-mediators may use their legal skills to evaluate the merits of arguments by lawyers representing the disputants, as discussed in previous chapters.[6]

Lawyer-mediators may face legal ethics issues if they convey the impression that they are representing one or both parties as if they were their lawyers.[7] For this reason, legal ethics authorities have said that lawyer-mediators may not give legal advice to unrepresented parties. Unless parties have counsel to review draft agreements, any mediator assistance in drafting settlement agreements should be limited to what non-attorneys could provide — such as writing out what the parties have agreed to do (Cole et al., 2014–2015, §§ 10:12-7).

OVER-PROMISING

To protect consumers, legislatures and ethics authorities have prohibited some practices associated with advertising mediation services or otherwise describing a mediator's role or competence (Cole et al., 2014–2015, § 10:8). For example, lawyer-mediators may face ethical issues if they suggest that disputants achieve the same results for less money by hiring a lawyer-mediator rather than their own independent counsel. In fact, lawyer-mediators must explain the unique role that independent counsel plays (ABA Model Rules of Professional Conduct 2.4, 2002). Mediators who are not lawyers may be warned or even charged with unauthorized practice of law if they advertise that their services can replace the need for lawyers (Cole et al., 2014–2015, § 10:10-14). In addition, the Model Standards for Mediators caution that any promises of dual professional roles can be problematic (Model Standards of Conduct for Mediators, Standard VI.A.5, 2005). The requirement for honesty by the mediator extends as well to qualifications to mediate (Uniform Mediation Act § 9(c), 2001;

---

[6]For a discussion of additional ethical issues for lawyers setting up a mediation practice, see Cole et al. (2014–2015, § 10:9).

[7]Though ABA Model Rule of Professional Conduct 5.7 indicates that mediation is not necessarily the practice of law, a lawyer-mediator is still governed by these rules in some respects.

Model Standards of Conduct for Mediators, Standards IV, VI, & VII, 2005).

Enforcement of Legal Standards

Legal standards are enforced through a variety of mechanisms. For example, a mediator who makes a prohibited recommendation to the court might be found to have breached a contract promising confidentiality and made to pay for the damages that caused. Or that mediator might have violated a state mediator ethics code, leading to a state ethics enforcement proceeding (in a few states only) to discipline the mediator. Or a mediation participant could sue that mediator for malpractice, though this happens extremely rarely (and mediators are often either immune from malpractice judgments or carry malpractice insurance). A different array of options might be available if a mediation participant blurts out what someone said during mediation in violation of the privilege, court rule, or order, or confidentiality agreement. These include: exclusions of the blurted-out statements from evidence, court sanctions against the disputant, allowing the other disputant to refute, and damages for breach of contract.

Preservation of the Disputants' Free Choice Regarding Whether to Settle in Mediation

Lawmakers seek to protect the disputants' free choice between settling in mediation and continuing in the legal process. They do this chiefly by limiting settlement pressures that would heavily burden the choice to begin or continue litigation or administrative proceedings. For example, the Uniform Mediation Act prohibits, unless the parties agree otherwise, mediators from making recommendations or reports based on the content of mediation to the judge assigned to the case in the event that the disputants do not settle (Uniform Mediation Act § 7, 2001). That prohibition precludes mediators from credibly threatening to make a particular report to the judge if a headstrong disputant does not settle.

Some laws go so far as to encourage *informed* choice. Disputants can bring counsel or another person to mediation, and the mediator cannot exclude those persons in states adopting the Uniform Mediation Act. This is true even if the parties have signed waivers of this protection in advance of the mediation. This law is aimed particularly at the practice of including waivers of counsel in the fine print of employment or consumer contracts (Uniform Mediation Act § 10, 2001).

Mediation Quality Enhancement

When a court or public agency refers disputants to mediation or the public funds a mediation program, lawmakers seek to improve the quality of that mediation. For example, they may impose entry-level mediator qualifications; continuing education and evaluation of mediators; and procedures and criteria for mediator selection. Outside this public setting, these quality-enhancing regulations are rare. In other words, people can commonly offer to mediate in the private sector without meeting qualifications or securing a license or permission to do so.

ENTRY-LEVEL MEDIATOR QUALIFICATIONS

Laws regarding who may mediate within publicly supported mediation programs commonly require mediation training. Sometimes these laws also require mediators to have specified educational degrees, professional licenses, experience, expertise in the law related to particular kinds of disputes, and demonstrated skills. The most extensive mediation training requirements tend to be for domestic relations mediation because many domestic relations parties attend mediation without lawyers. Additionally, these mediators are often tasked with looking out for the children's best interests and dealing appropriately with victims of intimate partner violence (Cole et al., 2014–2015, §§ 11:2-8).

CONTINUING EDUCATION AND EVALUATION

Some authorities are beginning to recognize that ongoing improvement in skills and additional reflection on a mediator's professional obligations may contribute more to the quality of mediators than do entry-level qualifications. These authorities might accept low levels of mediator training — perhaps 40 class hours — and not require any particular educational background or expertise, but use co-mediation or active supervision as a means to improve and ensure quality.

An office in Maryland's highest court designed a new approach to mediator qualifications consistent with research indicating that mediation experience is a more powerful indicator of high quality than are training, educational degree, or legal expertise related to the subject matter of the dispute (Wissler, 2002, pp. 699–700; Wissler, 2006, p. 133). That office created a set of standards for listing mediators on its roster, but did not require that courts use only mediators from its roster. Mediators could be listed on the roster with minimal mediation training, but had to commit to extensive continuing education, ongoing evaluation, and adherence to ethics rules. A number of Maryland's lower courts required their mediators to be on that roster, thus giving force of law to a low entry-level-requirement but continuous-improvement model (Rogers, Bordone, Sander & McEwen, 2013, pp. 158–161).

PROCEDURES AND CRITERIA FOR CASE SELECTION

A case-exclusion approach is premised on a lack of confidence that mediators, regardless of preparation, can assure a high quality and fair mediation for some kinds of disputes or disputants. An intimidated disputant provides an example of such cases. For this reason, a number of states preclude mandatory mediation of cases involving intimate partner violence (Adkins, 2010, p. 101), though other states continue to allow mediation with the use of special procedures such as meeting with parties in separate rooms, providing a support person for the victim, and assuring that the parties leave at staggered times. Another example is a case in which mediation would be a waste of time; the dispute needs to be litigated. To deal with such cases, a state might provide the right to opt out of mediation without giving a reason, or the opportunity to persuade the court that particular circumstances warrant by-passing mediation.

Protecting the Justice System's Role and Reputation

To avoid the appearance of judges directing mediation fees to cronies, some courts set standards and procedures for mediator selection and fees (Beckwith, 2011, pp. 357–361; Brazil, 1999, pp. 747–748). They may also set timetables and fees to protect the fairness of the justice system. The U.S. Court of Appeals for the First Circuit, for example, reversed a trial judge's referral to mediation that did not cap the mediator's fees or limit the required time in mediation, saying that both are required to ensure fairness. The Court commented, "The figures that have been bandied about in the briefs – $900 per hour or $9,000 per mediation day – are quite large and should not be left to the mediator's whim" (In re Atlantic Pipe Corp., 304 F.3d 136, 147 (1st Cir. 2002)).

Conclusion

Mediation-related law contains an underlying logic that facilitates the task of anticipating legal issues. Lawmakers tend to support use of mediation as long as that support does not undermine other important policies, and as long as it preserves fairness and public respect for the justice system. When there is a public connection to mediation, such as public funding or court referral, lawmakers also aim to enhance the integrity and quality of mediation.

Mediators should check the applicable law when mediating a new type of case or when mediating or anticipating future use of mediation communications in an unfamiliar jurisdiction. A mediator should also be alert to changes in mediation-related law. (The same caution applies to lawyers who represent participants in mediation.)

By joining local and national professional mediation and ADR organizations, both mediators and lawyers can keep abreast of changes and, if they choose, play a role in the development of mediation-related law.

References

Adkins, M. (2010). Moving out of the 1990s: An argument for updating protocol on divorce mediation in domestic abuse cases. *Yale Journal on Law & Feminism*, 22, 97.

American Arbitration Association, American Bar Association, & Association for Conflict Resolution. (2005). *Model standards of conduct for mediators.* Retrieved from http://www.americanbar.org/content/dam/aba/migrated/dispute/documents/model_standards_conduct_april2007.authcheckdam.pdf

American Bar Association. (1983). Model rules of professional conduct. Retrieved from http://www.americanbar.org/groups/professional_responsibility/ publications/model_rules_of_professional_conduct/model_rules_of_professional_ conduct_table_of_contents.html

Beckwith, S. (2011). District court mediation programs: A view from the bench. *Ohio State Journal on Dispute Resolution, 26*, 357–362.

Brazil, W. (1999). Comparing structures of the delivery of ADR services by courts: Critical values and concerns. *Ohio State Journal on Dispute Resolution, 14*, 715–811.

Brazil, W. (2000). Continuing the conversation about the current status and future of ADR: A view from the courts. *Journal of Dispute Resolution, 11*, 11–40.

Cole, S. R., McEwen, C. A., Rogers, N. H., Coben, J. R., & Thompson, P. N. (2014). *Mediation: Law, policy & practice* (2014–2015 ed.). Eagan, MN: Thomson Reuters.

In re Atlantic Pipe Corp., 304 F.3d 136, 147 (1st Cir. 2002).

Isaacson v. Isaacson, 792 A.2d 525, 533-536 (App. Div. 2002).

Kovach, K. (1997). Good faith in mediation – Requested, recommended, or required? A new ethic. *South Texas Law Review, 38*, 575–624.

Lande, J. (2002). Using dispute systems design methods to promote good-faith participation in court-connected mediation programs. *UCLA Law Review, 50*, 69–141.

Moffitt, M. (2003). Ten ways to get sued: A guide for mediators. *Harvard Negotiation Law Review, 8*, 81–132.

Nolan-Haley, J. (2013). *Alternative dispute resolution in a nutshell* (4th ed.). Eagan, MN: West.

Riskin, L. (1991). The represented client in a settlement conference: The lessons of G. Heileman Brewing Co., v. Joseph Oat Corp. *Washington University Law Review, 69*, 1059–1116.

Rogers, N. H., Bordone, R. C., Sander, F. E. A., & McEwen, C. A. (2013). *Designing systems and processes for managing disputes*. New York, NY: Wolters Kluwer.

Scanlon, K. M. (1999). *Mediator's deskbook*. New York, NY: CPR Institute for Dispute Resolution.

Sherman, E. (1993). Court-mandated alternative dispute resolution: What form of participation should be required? *Southern Methodist University Law Review, 46*, 2079–2112.

State v. Castellano, 460 So.2d 480 (Fla. App. 1984).

The Symposium on Standards of Practice. (2001). *Model standards of practice for family and divorce mediation*. Retrieved from http://www.americanbar.org/ content/dam/aba/migrated/family/reports/mediation.authcheckdam.pdf

Thompson, P. (2011). Good faith mediation in the federal courts. *Ohio State Journal on Dispute Resolution, 26*, 363–428.

Uniform Law Commissioners, & American Bar Association's Section on Dispute Resolution. (2001, amended in 2003). Uniform mediation act. Retrieved from http://www.uniformlaws.org/Act.aspx?title=Mediation%20Act

Wise, R. K. (2006). Mediation in Texas: Can the judge really make me do that? *South Texas Law Review, 47,* 849–880.

Wissler, R. (2002). Court-connected mediation in general civil cases: What we know from empirical research. *Ohio State Journal on Dispute Resolution, 17,* 641–703.

Wissler, R. (2006). The role of antecedent and procedural characteristics in mediation: A review of the research. In M. S. Herrman (Ed.), *Handbook of mediation: Bridging theory, research, and practice* (pp. 129–147). Malden, MA: Blackwell Publishing Ltd.

6 So You'd Like to Be a Mediator? ☆

If you think being a mediator could be a rewarding career, you are not alone. Experienced mediators often express the pleasure they receive in assisting parties to resolve their disputes. Craig McEwen described it this way:

> [I get great] satisfaction helping people work through problems to a resolution that they are able to accept, and that enables them to get on with their lives. So it is both the fascination of looking into their lives, and the sense that I had some impact on those lives that I find satisfying. (Craig McEwen, Professor of Political Economy and Sociology, Bowdoin College, Brunswick, ME)

Peter Adler described his excitement when the likely resolution of a hard-fought conflict becomes apparent:

> When ... people gain clarity into something that was one-dimensional for them, and then all of a sudden they can see that there are more dimensions than one, people start to get unstuck. I just love that. ... It's the golden moment for me when people are ready to move on

☆The text of this chapter has been adapted from Chapter 10 of Goldberg, Sander, Rogers, and Cole (2012). The quoted remarks of experienced mediators originally appeared in Shaw and Goldberg (2010).

from something they were tripping over in their lives. (Peter Adler, mediator; strategic public policy consultant, Honolulu, HI)

Bernie Mayer described the opportunities his mediation career has provided for personal growth and challenge:

We got involved in some really interesting projects in different parts of the world ... I began to explore new ways of dealing with family issues ... adoption, and child protection. So it was always changing... challenging, and there was always new stuff. (Bernie Mayer, Professor, Werner Institute for Negotiation and Dispute Resolution at Creighton University; Partner, CDR Associates, Boulder, CO)

Marcia Greenbaum talked about how important it is to her that her work is socially valuable:

I think that mediation is an opportunity to provide some kind of justice in the workplace, a compassionate ear to employees, supervisors and managers who have problems that a mediator might be able to help them resolve. So it is a way to contribute to the social good, and bring some peace to a workplace that might otherwise be less friendly or more hostile. (Marcia Greenbaum, labor and employment mediator, Essex, MA)

Mediation is a challenging, rewarding, and socially beneficial career. But, before you become committed to a mediation career, you need to be realistic. It is easy to get training; you can even start with a free online course. It is more difficult to find opportunities to gain experience mediating. Volunteering as a community mediator is a possibility, but there are already an estimated 20,000 volunteer mediators serving in approximately 400 community mediation centers, and many cities have no community mediation programs (Rhudy, 2014).

It is even more difficult to make mediation a full-time career. Most mediators have a "day job," typically as a lawyer, and mediate part-time. There are approximately 5,000 lawyers who also offer mediation and other dispute resolution services in addition to the practice of law (lawyers.com; martindale. com).

Serving as a mediator is not limited to lawyers. Many family therapists do some mediation. So do college and university professors who mediate disputes related to their area of expertise, for example labor and employment, construction, and environment. Former political office holders may be called upon to mediate public disputes. Former President Jimmy Carter (founder of the Carter Center, which seeks to find peaceful solutions to international conflicts), and former U.S. Senator George Mitchell (Northern Ireland Peace Process) are well-known examples, but there are many others at the local, state, national, and even international levels.

Most full-time mediators did not start out as full-time mediators. Mediation is their second or third career. Many began their professional careers as lawyers, and after many years of practice, they started mediating, transitioning gradually into full-time mediation, or, upon retiring from the practice of law, began mediating as a second career. Others went from practicing law to becoming a judge, and then became a mediator after retiring from the bench.

Another route to a career in mediation is to develop expertise in a nonlegal area, such as construction, environmental regulation, employee relations, or family therapy. Then, after receiving training in mediation, you can offer your services as a mediator in the area in which you are specialized.

Recently, more and more people are taking a direct path into mediation, one in which mediation is a first career, rather than a second or third career. The career biographies on the blog, "ADR as a 1st Career" (2014) show that those who choose a direct path to a mediation career are entrepreneurial, passionate, and dedicated to mediation. In order to launch themselves on their mediation career paths, they have volunteered and served as interns in state and local agencies that provide mediation (or other ADR) services, as well as in courts and nonprofit agencies that provide similar services. Ultimately, they have succeeded in making mediation a central element of their work lives, if not a full-time job. In addition to mediating, they direct mediation clinics, do mediation training, teach mediation, serve as organizational ombudsmen, etc. As Prof Alyson Carrel, the convener of the ADR as a 1st Career blog, has written, "Choosing ADR as your first career may not be easy, you may not be on the fast track to making millions, but if you are passionate about this work, it is possible" (Hinshaw, 2014).

Still interested in being a mediator? Here's how to get started.

Determine If You Have the Skills to Be a Successful Mediator

Do a self-assessment, comparing your skills to those of the best mediators (Goldberg & Shaw, 2007; Goldberg, Shaw, & Brett, 2009). The key to being a successful mediator, according to lawyers and others who represent clients in mediation, is the ability to gain the trust and confidence of the disputing parties. They say mediators do this by:

- being friendly, empathic, respectful, and caring;
- demonstrating high integrity through honesty, neutrality, fairness, and respecting confidentiality;
- being smart, well-prepared, and understanding the issues.

Also important to mediator success are:

- being patient/persistent — "She never quits";
- asking good questions and listening carefully to the responses;
- providing useful case outcome evaluations (particularly important for former judges who are mediating disputes that may be litigated if mediation does not lead to agreement).

What is striking about this short list of key skills is that, with the exception of providing useful case outcome evaluations, anyone who genuinely wants to become a mediator should be able to learn them.

Take a Basic Training Course in Mediation

Basic mediation training courses are offered in nearly every part of the country. The most important reason for taking such a course is to find out if mediation is what you thought it was and if you enjoy doing it. For that reason, you'll want to choose a course that gives you experience mediating simulated disputes. Even better is a course that also lets you observe real mediations and prepares you to actually mediate. One experienced mediator and mediation trainer said:

If, after your basic training in mediation, you are still interested and believe that you have the ability to succeed, further training and experience are in order. Ideally, but not necessarily, this further training and experience will be in a field that particularly appeals to you. Some community mediation programs train mediators and then use them as volunteer mediators, as do some court-connected small-claims mediation programs. [B]e a volunteer mediator in a small claims court or community mediation setting, because ... you need to figure out how you fit in the coat of a mediator. Even if your goal is to mediate different topics, practice is important. We each have different strengths and we mediate in different ways and so you learn by doing. (Gail Bingham, Environmental Mediator, President Emeritus, RESOLVE, Washington, DC)

Get the Right Credentials

If you want a mediation career in which a substantial portion of your practice will be mediating disputes that will otherwise end up in litigation, going to law school will provide a valuable credential. Initially, it should provide you with a deep understanding of the litigation process. In addition, it is typically the parties' lawyers who select the mediator in disputes that involve pending litigation, and the lawyers tend to believe that the mediator in such a dispute must have a firm grasp of the relevant law. Indeed, lawyers may search for a mediator who is not only a lawyer, but also a judge who has retired from the bench to pursue a mediation career. The classic advice to a young lawyer aspiring to a career as mediator is "practice law, become a judge, retire, and then mediate."

As mediation becomes more widely used as a dispute resolution method, a deep understanding of the context in which the dispute arises may be as valuable a credential as a law degree. For example, a degree (and experience) in social work, counseling, or psychology may lead to a career mediating family issues. Similarly, a degree in environmental studies and experience with environmental issues can lead to a career mediating environmental disputes. (A law degree combined with experience in one of these fields is another pathway to a career as a mediator.)

Mediators may also have degrees in conflict resolution. Such degrees are increasingly offered at the graduate level, at times on a stand-alone basis, at times as part of a joint degree in conflict resolution and law.

Seek a Mentor

Another way to get experience as a mediator is to develop a relationship with someone who can mentor you. Choose a mentor who has a successful ADR career in your field of interest and is willing to give you advice. Ideally, this person will allow you to observe her at work, and will discuss with you the tactics and strategies she uses to try to help the parties settle their dispute. Observing your mentor at work and discussing strategy with her might even develop into a relationship in which she would allow you to co-mediate with her.

Market Your Services

Consider all the ways that you can alert potential clients that you will be offering mediation services. This may include developing your own website, sending announcements, making telephone calls, and using social media. If you have previously worked in a particular sector, such as health care or elder care, in which you can claim some expertise, be certain to advertise your mediation services in that sector. See if there are local, state, or national lists of mediators on which you might have your name appear. Get active in your local professional organizations, where you might meet people who could recommend your services. Use social media to comment on a current or past dispute that has stirred local interest, emphasizing how a mediator might attempt to resolve this conflict.

If you are an attorney, be alert to the ethical standards for lawyers discussed in Chapter 5 regarding being truthful in advertising. Be careful not to mislead potential clients about your qualifications, skills, or experience. Your advertising may not promise a mediation settlement, but you may report the proportion of settlements in cases that you have mediated. You may also refer to people and organizations for whom you have mediated, if you have their permission to do so. (Even if you are not an attorney, you would be well-advised to abide by ethical standards similar to those for attorneys.)

Your marketing should be part of your overall business plan. One useful guide for developing your mediation practice is *The Mediation Career Guide* (Mosten, 2001).

Keep Up with Developments in Mediation

One way to keep up with developments in the field is to join the Association for Conflict Resolution (ACR), which is the professional association for mediators and other conflict resolution professionals. ACR membership is open to non-lawyers, as well as lawyers. At ACR meetings you can share experiences with other aspiring and successful ADR practitioners and learn from them. ACR has local chapters, as well as sections focusing on particular types of mediation that may be of interest to you. Among these are the sections on environment and public policy, health care, online disputes, workplace disputes, and many others.

In addition to ACR, there is the Section on Dispute Resolution of the American Bar Association. Nearly half the members of the Section on Dispute Resolution are non-lawyers (M. Buckley, personal communication, January 17, 2015), so even if you are not a lawyer, don't let that stop you from joining this group. For community mediators, there is the National Association for Community Mediation; and for family mediators, particularly those working on family issues in the courts, there is the Association of Family and Conciliation Courts.

Another way to keep up with developments in mediation is by reading, either online or off. There are many blogs that cover mediation as well as other ADR topics. For a list of some of those blogs, see the list of ADR blogs at the end of this chapter.

There are also many ADR publications that cover mediation, including *Dispute Resolution Magazine* (ABA Section of Dispute Resolution); *Dispute Resolution Journal* (American Arbitration Association); *World Arbitration and Mediation Report* (Transnational Juris Publications); *Alternatives* (CPR Institute); *Negotiation Journal* (Blackwell); *Ohio State Journal on Dispute Resolution*; *Harvard Negotiation Law Review*; *Journal of Dispute Resolution* (University of Missouri-Columbia);

Conflict Resolution Quarterly (Jossey-Bass), and *Family Court Review* (Association of Family and Conciliation Courts).

Mediate in Your Everyday Life

Once you begin to learn about mediation, you will see many opportunities in your work and personal life to use your developing mediation skills. Particularly if you are a manager, you might use these skills to assist subordinates or even peers to resolve disputes. If you have the opportunity to sit in on a mediation in which your organization is involved, take advantage of this experience to learn how mediation looks from the perspective of the disputants.

Engaging in informal mediation with friends and family is also possible, but runs the risk of harming your relationship with one or both of the disputants if they are dissatisfied with the outcome of your informal mediation. Thus, instead of mediating yourself, you might do better to explain mediation and advise them how to locate a mediator.

Don't Quit Your Day Job

Don't quit your day job is advice that experienced mediators have been giving to aspiring mediators for decades. A somewhat more nuanced version would advise you not to cut your ties with a steady, income-producing job until you have done enough mediation or mediation-related work that you can be reasonably certain of a steady stream of mediation or mediation-related income.

References

Goldberg, S. B., & Shaw, M. L. (2007). The secrets of successful (and unsuccessful) mediators continued: Studies two and three. *Negotiation Journal, 23,* 393–418.

Goldberg, S. B., Shaw, M. L., & Brett, J. M. (2009). What difference does a robe make? Comparing mediators with and without prior judicial experience. *Negotiation Journal, 25,* 277–305.

Goldberg, S. B., Sander, F. E. A., Rogers, N. H., & Cole, S. R. (2012). *Dispute resolution: Negotiation, mediation, arbitration, and other processes.* New York, NY: Walters Kluwer.

Hinshaw, A. (2014, December 11). Carrel – ADR as first career video blog update [blog post]. Retrieved from http://www.indisputably.org/?p=6170

Mediation, U. S. (n.d.). http://www.martindale.com/Results.aspx

Mediation lawyers. (n.d.). http://www.lawyers.com/mediation/all-cities/all-states/lawyers/?ac=6|1

Mosten, F. S. (2001). *The mediation career guide*. San Francisco, CA: Jossey-Bass

Rhudy, R. J. (2014). *Engaging conflict for fun and profit: Current and emerging career trends in conflict resolution*. Maryland Mediation and Conflict Resolution Office (MACRO). Retrieved from http://www.courts.state.md.us/macro/pdfs/reports/currentemergingcareertrends.pdf

Shaw, M. L., & Goldberg, S. B. (2010). Who wants to be a mediator? *Dispute Resolution Magazine, 16*, 24–29.

Links to Organizations and Journals of Interest

Alternatives (CPR Institute): http://www.cpradr.org/EventsEducation/Alternatives.aspx

Association for Conflict Resolution (ACR): https://www.imis100us2.com/ACR/ACR/Default.aspx?hkey=6d51647b-e4cd-49d5-bc8a-36a4773a9054&WebsiteKey=a9a587d8-a6a4-4819-9752-ef5d3656db55

Association of Family and Conciliation Courts: www.afccnet.org

Cardozo Journal of Conflict Resolution: http://cardozojcr.com

Conflict Resolution Quarterly: http://onlinelibrary.wiley.com/journal/10.1002/%28ISSN%291541-1508

Dispute Resolution Journal: http://www.jurispub.com/cart.php?m=product_detail&p=10589

Dispute Resolution Magazine: http://www.americanbar.org/publications/dispute_resolution_magazine.html

Family Court Review: http://onlinelibrary.wiley.com/journal/10.1111/%28ISSN%291744-1617

Harvard Negotiation Law Review: http://www.hnlr.org/

Journal of Dispute Resolution: http://law.missouri.edu/csdr/journal/

National Association for Community Mediation: www.nafcm.org

Negotiation Journal: http://onlinelibrary.wiley.com/journal/10.1111/%28ISSN%291571-9979

Ohio State Journal on Dispute Resolution: http://moritzlaw.osu.edu/students/groups/osjdr/

Pepperdine Dispute Resolution Journal: http://law.pepperdine.edu/dispute-resolution-law-journal/

Section on Dispute Resolution of the American Bar Association: http://www.americanbar.org/groups/dispute_resolution.html

The Yearbook on Arbitration and Mediation: https://pennstatelaw.psu.edu/_file/YAM/YAM_Winter_2012.pdf

World Arbitration and Mediation Report: http://www.jurispub.com/cart.php?m=product_detail&p=6554

Suggested Reading

Carrel, A. (2014). ADR as a first career [blog]. Retrieved from http://www.adras1stcareer.blogspot.com/

Finding Opportunities. (2015). *Dispute Resolution Magazine*, (Spring), 4–33.

Stories. (2014). *ACR Magazine*, *13*(4), 6–29. http://www.acresolution-digital.org/acresolutionmag/fall_2014#pg4

Hoffman, D. A., & Boston Law Collaborative (2013). *Mediation: A practice guide for mediators, lawyers, and other professionals*. Boston, MA: Massachusetts Continuing Legal Education Inc.

Lenski, T. (2008). *Making mediation your day job*. Bloomington, IN: iUniverse.

Lovenheim, P. (2002). *Becoming a mediator: An insider's guide to exploring careers in mediation*. San Francisco, CA: Jossey-Bass.

Mosten, F. S. (2001). *The mediation career guide*. San Francisco, CA: Jossey-Bass.

Rhudy, R. J. (2014). *Engaging conflict for fun and profit: Current and emerging career trends in conflict resolution*. Maryland Mediation and Conflict Resolution Office (MACRO). Retrieved from http://www.courts.state.md.us/macro/pdfs/reports/currentemergingcareertrends.pdf

Velikonja, U. (2009). Making peace and making money: Economic analysis of the market for mediators in private practice. *Albany Law Review*, *72*, 257–291.

ADR blogs

Title	Authors	Description
ADR as a First Career	Alyson Carrel	This video blog is a place to share and read about individuals who chose to begin their professional career in the ADR field. Typically, ADR is seen as a 2nd (or 3rd) career. But as more and more law schools, graduate schools, undergraduate schools, and even high schools, are teaching students about mediation and dispute resolution in general, individuals are graduating and looking to begin their career in ADR from the start. They don't want to wait and do something else before they have an opportunity to do what they love (http://adras1stcareer.blogspot.com/).
American Bar Association	Peter Arcese and Richard Lord	The ABA Mediation Committee studies the many applications of mediation, and promotes the utilization of mediation and its development as a substantive practice area. The Committee assists with the understanding and uses of mediation, and offers members ways to incorporate mediation into their practice (http://apps. americanbar.org/dch/committee.cfm?com= DR020500).
Brains on Purpose	Stephanie Allen and Jeffrey Schwartz	Stephanie West Allen, JD, practiced law in California for several years, held offices in local bar associations, and wrote chapters for California Continuing Education of the Bar. While in CA, Stephanie completed a number of five-day mediation training programs, including several with the Center for Mediation in Law, and a two-year intensive with Center cofounder Gary Friedman. She has been a mediator for over two and one-half decades (http:// www.gerryriskin.com/new-blog-brains-on-purpose/).
Business Conflict Blog	Peter Phillips	F. Peter Phillips is a commercial arbitrator and mediator with substantial experience providing consultation on the management of business disputes to companies around the globe. Mr. Phillips served for nearly 10 years as Senior Vice

(Continued)

Title	Authors	Description
		President of the International Institute for Conflict Prevention and Resolution (CPR Institute). During that time, he earned a reputation as an author, teacher, industry liaison, and systems designer for the avoidance, management, and resolution of complex and sophisticated business conflicts (http://www. businessconflictmanagement.com/blog/).
Business Mediation Network	Paul Simon	Proposes business-like solutions for business disputes (http:// businessmediationnetwork.com/blog/).
CPR Institute	Multiple	The International Institute for Conflict Management and Prevention (commonly known as the CPR Institute) News & Podcasts provides resources including: articles by a variety of authors; model clauses; blog entries, indexed by topic; and podcasts to prepare for dispute resolution practice internationally (http://www. cpradr.org/RulesCaseServices.aspx).
Dispute Resolution Counsel	Founding Member Michael Zeytoonian	Dispute Resolution Counsel presents ideas, concepts, and progressive alternative dispute resolution (ADR) practices that facilitate our vision of "Resolution without Litigation." This blog is primarily for parties to a dispute and practitioners, providing practical insights on how these processes can be best used to give clients value. We will also explore the evolution of collaborative practice and the increased use of settlement counsel as efficient and cost effective means to resolve disputes, without the collateral damage of the adversarial approaches. See more at: http:// disputeresolutioncounsel.com/blog/ #sthash.xr9pPMiB.dpuf
Disputing Blog	Karl Bayer	Disputing is published by Karl Bayer, a dispute resolution expert based in Austin, Texas. Articles published on Disputing aim to provide original insight and commentary around issues related to arbitration, mediation, and the alternative dispute resolution industry (http://www. disputingblog.com/category/mediation/).

(Continued)

Title	Authors	Description
Indisputably .org	Multiple	Professors comment on mediation and arbitration, both theory and practice (http://www.indisputably.org/).
JAMS ADR Blog	CEO Chris Poole	The JAMS ADR blog serves to engage our clients, the legal community and the public in a discussion about alternative dispute resolution. As leaders and experts in mediation, arbitration, and more, it's our duty to remain at the forefront of legal developments, trends, and news in areas of law that pertain to ADR (http://jamsadrblog.com/).
Just Court ADR	Resolution Systems Institute Executive Director Susan Yates	Discusses current issues in court alternative dispute resolution, hopefully bringing fresh, unique perspectives to these topics. RSI's mission is to strengthen justice by enhancing court ADR systems through expertise in program development, research, and resources. RSI focuses on court-related ADR because the justice system is where people usually turn when they are in conflict. Working in Illinois and nationally, RSI gathers and disseminates reliable information about court ADR, conducts analyses of court ADR program models, and builds networks among interested individuals and organizations. RSI also assists courts and communities in establishing mediation programs and determining how to monitor and evaluate them (http://blog.aboutrsi.org/).
Kluwer Mediation Blog	Editors Nadja Alexander and Bill Marsh	Kluwer Mediation Blog (KMB) is a publication of Kluwer Law International providing information, news and updates on mediation around the globe. We have gathered together leading international experts to report on the latest developments. The result is a fresh, high-quality, and timely examination of the world of international mediation (http://kluwermediationblog.com/).
Mediate.com	CEO – Jim Melamed Managing Editor – Clare Fowler	With over 15,000 articles, news items, blog postings, and videos, and over 5 million annual visitor sessions, Mediate.com is the world's leading mediation website. Mediate.com serves as a bridge

(*Continued*)

Title	Authors	Description
		between professionals offering mediation services and people needing mediation services (http://www.mediate.com/index.cfm).
Mediate-LA	Joseph Markowitz	Joe Markowitz has served as a mediator for more than 15 years, has written and spoken extensively about mediation, has taken countless courses and seminars in mediation, and is a member of the Mediation Panels in both the District Court and Bankruptcy Court in the Central District of California, as well as the Los Angeles County Superior Court. He is currently the President of the Southern California Mediation Association, and headed the SCMA's task force establishing a "Select a Mediator" program in response to the closure of the LA Superior Court mediation program. He also served for 2 years on the Superior Court's ADR committee (http://www.mediate-la.com/).
Negotiation Law Blog	Victoria Pynchon	I blog on negotiation here, where I pay attention to the settlement of legal disputes, and at She Negotiates, where I pay attention to the benefits to and challenges of women negotiating on their own behalves as well as on behalf of those they love and care about (http://www.negotiationlawblog.com/mediation-in-car-accident-cases-can-lead-to-equitable-settlement-of-claims/).
The Mediation Channel	Diane Levin	This blog delivers news, musings, tips, and information on alternative dispute resolution and people-focused innovations in the practice of law (https://mediationchannel.com/).
The Mediation Times	Amanda Bucklow	I mediate internationally and believe that mediation belongs at the heart of our businesses and organizations because it crosses borders, both cultural and geographical. Mediation is a process that can be flexed enough to deliver what people need in a way that the legal process cannot. Mediation is a natural companion to the legal system

(*Continued*)

Title	Authors	Description
		(http://blog.amandabucklow.co.uk/editor-amanda-bucklow/).
Transformative Mediation	Dan Simon	The mission of the Institute for the Study of Conflict Transformation is to study and promote the understanding of conflict processes (http://www.transformativemediation.org/blog-list/blog/).

Index

provision of mediators by, 18
Mediator(s)
appearance of bias, avoiding, 28
BATNA, aiding parties to evaluate, 51–54
becoming, 97–104
coaching the parties, 43–44
confidentiality, mediator responsibility, 83–85
conflicts of interest, 87–88
continuing education and evaluation, 91–92
credentials, 101–102
disclosure by, 22, 35–37
entry-level qualifications, 91
ethical standards, 77–93
fees, 23, 88
first career, mediation as, 99
goal, 59–62
guidelines for conducting separate sessions, 32–34
impartiality of, 87–90
integrity of, 87–90
listening, active, 37–38
marketing of services, 102–103
mentors, 102
mixed professional practices, 89
Model Standards of Conduct for Mediators, 83–84, 87–90
Model Standards of Practice for Family and Divorce Mediation, 84
proposals, 48–50, 71–72
provision of by mediation service firms and courts, 18
quality, 91–92
questioning, 35–37
rewards of serving as, 97–98
role of, 27
selection of, 21–22

success, keys to, 27, 100
training courses, 100–101
unfair tentative agreement, dealing with, 74
warning to parties of termination of mediation, 71
Mitchell, George, 99
Mixed professional practices, 89
Model Standards of Conduct for Mediators, (see Mediators)
Model Standards of Practice for Family and Divorce Mediation, (see Mediators)

National Association for Community Mediation, 103
Negotiation, 5–6, 11
distinguished from mediation, 19
failure of, 13
Negotiation Journal, 103
Non-precedent setting agreements, 47
No separate sessions, 34

Ohio State Journal on Dispute Resolution, 103
Opening statements, 30
Ordering issues, 30–31
Over-promising, 89–90

Parties
ability to determine mediation procedures, 25
availability in mediation, ensuring, 28
behavioral issues, 67–69
best settlement proposals, encouraging, 50–51
bringing together for final settlement effort, 70–71
coaching of, 43–44

Printed in the United States
By Bookmasters